JOHN BENTON

# JOHN BENTON

 **EVANGELICAL PRESS**

EVANGELICAL PRESS
12 Wooler Street, Darlington, Co. Durham, DL1 1RQ, England

© Evangelical Press 1992
*First published 1992*

**British Library Cataloguing in Publication Data available**

ISBN 0 85234 294 2

Unless otherwise indicated, Scripture quotations in this publication are from the Holy Bible, New International Version. Copyright © 1973, 1978, 1984 International Bible Society. Published by Hodder & Stoughton.

Printed and Bound in Great Britain at Cox & Wyman Limited, Reading.

To my parents

Charles and Betty Benton

# Contents

1. Introduction — 11
2. One world — 13
3. One way — 22
4. Why only Jesus? — 40
5. Jesus and other religions — 48
6. The road to freedom — 71
Appendix I: The Bible's attitude to other religions — 93
Appendix II: The coming of the man of lawlessness — 101
References — 112

# Acknowledgements

Many people have been helpful to me in producing this book. First, I would like to express my thanks to the elders and deacons of Chertsey Street for the three-month sabbatical in the summer of 1991 during which most of this book was written. Secondly, I am indebted to my parents-in-law Alick and Laurie for giving me house room in Kidlington on a couple of occasions to work on this project. Lastly, and especially, thank you to Eileen Savage for her hard work and willingness in typing the manuscript.

John Benton
May 1992

When all the broken-hearted people
living in the world agree
there will be an answer
let it be

(Paul McCartney).

'The kingdom of heaven is like a merchant looking for fine pearls. When he found one of great value, he went away and sold everything he had and bought it'

(Matthew 13:45).

'Blessed are you when men hate you,
    when they exclude you and insult you
    and reject your name as evil,
    because of the Son of Man ...
But I tell you who hear me:
    Love your enemies,
    do good to those who hate you'

(Luke 6:22,27).

# 1.
# Introduction

'I am the way and the truth and the life. No one comes to the Father except through me' (John 14:6). There could be no more comprehensive and emphatic claim to be the sole means of bringing people to God than these words of Jesus Christ. Jesus covers all the options. He claims the way — the means of eternal salvation and the pattern of all religious activity which leads to God — is found in no one else but him and his example. He claims the truth — all certainty of what to believe about God and how to find God — is found exclusively in him and his teaching. He claims the life — all vital experience of being truly awake and alive to God — is found nowhere else but in him and his Spirit. Religion is ultimately worthwhile only as it leads to Christ.

The exclusive claims of Jesus have been reasserted by the church down the centuries. Personal redemption requires conscious faith in the Lord Jesus. The apostles declared concerning Christ: 'Salvation is found in no one else, for there is no other name under heaven given to men by which we must be saved' (Acts 4:12). 'God has given us eternal life, and this life is in his Son. He who has the Son has life; he who does not have the Son of God does not have life' (1 John 5:11-12).

Statements like these concerning Jesus have always been controversial. It was for making such assertions about himself and refusing to retract them that Jesus was crucified. His claims were repugnant to the religious and political hierarchy of his times. They reacted violently against him. However, the controversy continues even today and as we come to the end of the twentieth century and are about to enter the twenty-first after his death, it seems set to be engaged with renewed vigour.

What are people to make of the claims of Jesus? Are they simply misguided and outmoded statements no longer appropriate to the times? What are we to make of those who continue to believe these claims of Jesus? Do these claims to the exclusive way of salvation flow from mere arrogance and bigotry? Why is the controversy over these matters likely to become more acute in coming years? These are the kinds of questions considered in this book.

We will begin by taking up that last question.

# 2.
# One world

It appears that the argument concerning the exclusive claims of Jesus is likely to intensify in coming years because they cut across the direction of the modern world and the thoughts and aspirations of many who would see themselves as reasonable, peace-loving people.

It is probably true to say that the world has changed more radically in the last hundred years than in any previous era of history. Now a general direction to that change is beginning to emerge. We are living in momentous days: days in which not only is the world undergoing great transformations but in many ways it is coming together. The consensus vision of the future is that of *one world*, the unity of people and of nations. There is a tide in the affairs of men which is moving towards a unified world. We can see this if we stop and take stock of our times.

*Culturally* our world has come together enormously during the twentieth century. When Arnold Toynbee published his famous book *A study of history* in the 1930s he could still speak of four great world faiths and their cultures being located in different geographical regions of the world. That is no longer true. People have migrated. Education has caused ideas to travel. Eastern religions have come to the West, Western thought has been transported to the East and societies generally have become more secularized. The great cities of the world now tend to be rather the same — multi-cultural and cosmopolitan.

*Politically* we have, even in the last few years, witnessed the spectacular collapse of old-style Communism in Eastern Europe and Russia. The era of the two world systems of Communism versus capitalism seems to be over. There is also reason to hope that we are witnessing the fall of apartheid in South Africa. At the same time there is what seems to be the rise of an increasingly agreed ideology of democracy and personal freedom for the nations of the world. The 1991 Gulf War was marked by an unparalleled co-operation of countries through the United Nations and talk of the emergence of a 'new world order'.

Similarly *environmental issues* are forcing us more and more to look upon the world as a united whole. Car exhaust fumes in the developed countries and the burning of the Brazilian rain forests impinge upon all the earth through the so-called greenhouse effect produced by the resulting carbon dioxide. The damage to the ozone layer and the pollution of the oceans bring health risks to us all. Managing the environment on a global basis makes sense. The people of the earth are driven to collaborate on these matters.

*Economics* plays a part too. As we contemplate the riches of the Western hemisphere and the reality of poverty and recurring famine in the Third World, surely the day is not too far off when the solution will be seen to be not just European economic union, but a loose overall management of the world economy in order to iron out such tragic ambiguities. An economic plan for the world which did not stop the growth of developed countries and made sure that underdeveloped countries were at least looked after and their people provided for would certainly be fairer.

Also, of course, steps forward in *technology* have been steps towards making the vision of one world a reality. The revolutionary advances in computers and telecommunications

# One world

in our lifetime are actually providing the means by which the whole world can be instantly in touch with itself. These are some of the factors which are drawing the world together. One world seems to be the way for the next step in history.

## What kind of oneness?

People have tried to unify the world before. From Alexander the Great through the medieval popes to Adolf Hitler, leaders and generals have tried to conquer the world and bring it under one banner. But they have failed. Theirs has been the way of domination and totalitarianism, trying to impose a uniformity upon the world in order to achieve unity. But the genius of the present hour which draws the world together is different. It is the idea of pluralism or unity in diversity. Uniformity has been rejected and the spirit of 'live and let live' is finally predominating. This is the attitude of cultural pluralism which may be defined as 'the attitude which welcomes the variety of different cultures and lifestyles within one society and believes that this is an enrichment of human life'.[1] National aspirations, ethnic distinctives, self-determination and alternative lifestyles are not suppressed but encouraged and embraced within the community of mankind. Tolerance and understanding are surely no bad things, and generally speaking we must say that all this is right.\*

This, then, I suggest, is the *Zeitgeist*, or spirit of our time.

---

\* However, a caveat must be added. Cultures and lifestyles are not morally neutral and some are unacceptable. To take an extreme case in order to make the point, no one, presumably, would want to see cannibalism or slavery as welcome lifestyles in our towns and cities. All ways of life should be accepted and respected so long as they are morally acceptable to the rest of the community and respect basic human dignity. The question of where to draw the line on what is morally acceptable will, of course, be a problem. The Christian believes that it is a dilemma that can only be solved by the acknowledgement of God's laws.

To bring the world together in peace and mutual acceptance is an understandable aim and in many ways a commendable crusade. But what does this mean for the person who believes that Christ is the only way of salvation?

## Religious pluralism

'No one comes to the Father except by me,' said Jesus. Against this background of *cultural* pluralism there is increasing pressure for an outlook of *religious* pluralism to be adopted by us all. That is, that we should all accept that the differences between the religions are not a matter of truth and falsehood, but simply different perceptions of the one truth. Religious belief, it is said, is a private matter. No one should claim to know the truth about God. Each person should be left to his or her own opinion. No religion should insist on converting others to its way of thinking. Everything must be done to bring unity rather than division and the idea of absolute religious truth is looked upon as divisive and therefore expendable. It will always divide the world into the two camps of the converted and the unconverted. It is therefore rejected by the world.

The horrors of religious mob violence in certain parts of the world, and of terrorist activities seemingly motivated by 'fundamentalist' religious conviction in others, lend momentum to this argument. To claim to have the truth will inevitably divide the world into believers and non-believers and lead to antagonism. The idea that there is one absolute, right way, as opposed to wrong ways, in religious matters is viewed as a tremendous obstacle to world peace and stability. This is an indictment not just against Christianity, of course, but against any faith which claims to be the truth.

A letter which appeared in one of our local newspapers not so long ago expressed this view very forcefully: 'We are all

# One world

aware of the dangers of causing offence to the religious sensibilities of others. But surely we should also be concerned about offence caused by religious beliefs... Religious conviction remains the greatest cause of war, hate, atrocities and division in the world. There is no shortage of faith in the world, but a terrifying dearth of love... I recently attended an Anglican baptism from the Alternative Service Book... It unambiguously stated that unless we are "born again" ... we cannot enter the kingdom of God... My own children ... are being brought up to think of all humanity as their brothers and sisters, to have respect for all living things and they would find it inconceivable to be "saved" in the knowledge that any other human being was not... Religious intolerance is not inevitable... Despite appearances to the contrary there are numerous hopeful moves to establish understanding and respect between different religious traditions and there is a growing movement of those aware of the spiritual potential of humankind, but who reject all labels because of their concern for unity not division.'[2]

Thus the claim of the Lord Jesus Christ to be the one and only way to God is viewed with suspicion and even detestation by many people today. Christ's claims are described as a hindrance rather than a help to world peace and, as in the letter just quoted, they are rejected on these pragmatic grounds irrespective of any investigation into the evidence as to their truth or falsehood. Those who follow Christ are perceived as, at best, misguided and, at worst, narrow, arrogant and intolerant.

There, then, is the indictment against Christ and Christianity. Jesus' claim to be exclusively the way, the truth and the life is increasingly unacceptable to the modern world.

## Who is being tolerant?

What are we to make of these accusations? Perhaps to begin with we ought to consider this question of tolerance.

Sadly, those who make much of tolerance often prove to be highly intolerant of those who take a stand for Christ. The advocate of secularism often subconsciously operates with the following rather hypocritical conjugation in mind: 'I hold opinions; you are arrogant; he or she is bigoted.' The secularist may hold firm ideas, but if the Christian does, he or she is branded as a bigot. Our letter writer is like that. In one breath she said that all should be accepted, but the whole tone of her letter makes it clear that those who happen to believe in the uniqueness of Christ were not included in this. She was in fact just producing a pluralistic version of 'Accept my creed or else I can't accept you.'

The experience of one well-known American theologian, R. C. Sproul, reflects this intolerance towards Christians by the 'tolerant' and at the same time unlocks the nub of the argument concerning Christ as the only way. Sproul writes, 'One of the most embarrassing moments I have ever experienced came as a new student in the English class at college. It was a time of painful public humiliation. The professor was a former war correspondent who was outwardly hostile to Christianity. In the middle of the class she looked up at me and said, "Mr Sproul, do you believe that Jesus Christ is the only way to God?" I gasped as I felt the weight of her question, and knew that every eye in the room was on me. My mind raced for a way to escape my dilemma. I knew if I said "Yes" people would be angry. At the same time I knew that if I said "No" I would be denying what Jesus said of himself. Finally, I mumbled almost inaudibly, "Yes, I do." The teacher responded with unmitigated fury. She said in front of the whole class, "That's the most narrow-minded, bigoted and arrogant statement I have ever heard. You must be the supreme egotist to believe that your religion is the only way." I made no reply but slouched rather meekly in my chair.'

After the class was dismissed, Sproul went to talk to his teacher privately. He asked her if she thought that it was at least

## One world

theoretically possible that Christ is the only way to God. She allowed the possibility. He then asked if she thought it were possible that without being narrow-minded or bigoted a person might honestly come to believe that Jesus is God. She recognized that possibility too. Sproul went on to say, 'Do you see that it is possible for me to believe in the uniqueness of Christ because he taught it? If I believed that Christ is the only way because it is *my* way, that would be arrogance and egotism.' The English professor finally acknowledged all this and in fact went on to apologize for what she had said in the class. However, then she went on to raise a more serious problem: 'How can you believe in a God who only allows one way to himself? Isn't it narrow-minded of God to restrict redemption to one Saviour and one faith?'[3]

That is a fair question and in many ways it is the crux of all the controversy and we will face this question later. However, before we do that it is worth just underlining something. It needs to be emphasized that Christians are not trying to be arrogant or conceited in preaching that Jesus is the only way. They are simply seeking to be faithful to his claims in sharing their faith. And if any arrogance or bigotry does creep into the spirit of the church's proclamation, that is wrong. Our Master does want us to proclaim him as the sole Saviour of the world, but he expects us to do that humbly, respectfully and lovingly. If the church is to declare his message, it must be done his way, in his spirit.

Also it needs to be understood that as Christians, proclaiming Christ alone as the way to God, we are not against religious tolerance. Indeed, historically, it is the Protestant churches which have fostered the concept of freedom of conscience which provided the springboard from which the present religious tolerance in the Western world has developed. The U.S. Constitution, with its freedom of religion, is rooted in the nonconformist ideals of the Pilgrim Fathers and their descendants.

Under the principle of religious tolerance, all religious systems which respect human dignity are guaranteed freedom of expression and equal treatment under the law. That is right. Jesus firmly rejected any idea of his cause being promoted by violence or by the sword. 'Put your sword back in its place,' said Christ to Peter as he tried to defend Jesus from arrest by the authorities, 'for all who draw the sword will die by the sword' (Matthew 26:52). The kingdom of Christ is not of this world and can never be extended or defended by force. Jesus said, 'My kingdom is not of this world. If it were, my servants would fight to prevent my arrest by the Jews. But now my kingdom is from another place' (John 18:36). Freedom of thought and speech reflects the Christian view of the dignity of all human beings. Society should be big enough to embrace people of different religious persuasions. But it must be said that the fact that all religions are equally tolerated does not mean that all religions are equally true.†

Biblical Christianity finds its claim that Christ is the only way of salvation at odds with the mood of the modern world, and the crux of the problem is this question which Christians are asked: 'How can you believe in a God who only allows one way to himself?' The God of the Bible, who so loved the world

---

†A further issue could also be clarified briefly at this point. Bible Christianity and saving faith are the possession of no one Christian denomination. No Bible-believing Christian says that a person has to join that particular church in order to be saved. The Jehovah's Witnesses, by contrast, tell us that we must all become JWs or we are lost. As far as I understand, the Mormons believe that only their baptism procures salvation. Similarly, unfortunately, classical Roman Catholicism teaches that there is no salvation for anyone outside the fold of Rome. It is not true that people must join a particular Christian denomination in order to be saved. But true Christianity does point people to Christ — to Christ alone, who said, 'No one comes to the Father except through me' (John 14:6), and who said, 'If you do not believe that I am the one I claim to be you will die in your sins' (John 8:24). There is not only one denomination, but there is only one Saviour.

## One world

that he gave his only begotten Son that whoever believes in him will not perish but have everlasting life, is rejected as unloving and parsimonious. For there to be only one Saviour and one way of salvation is looked upon as unnecessarily restrictive and morally abhorrent. 'Your God is too narrow-minded,' Christians are told. In answer to all this we are going to look first at what the Bible says about there being only one way of salvation and then secondly consider briefly why we should believe it is true.

# 3.
# One way

Before we proceed, there are a number of things to be made clear concerning the Christian view of mankind.

First of all, the loving unity of mankind, so evidently yet to be achieved, is a fine quest and indeed is a biblical ideal. It is the Bible which teaches the equality of all people before God, their Maker. The idea of the 'family of man' springs from the Scripture teaching concerning the first human couple, named by the Bible as Adam and Eve. As their descendants, mankind, for all its diversity, is indeed one family, not many different families. The apostle Paul, preaching to the philosophers of first-century Athens, declared, 'From one man [God] made every nation of men, that they should inhabit the whole earth' (Acts 17:26). Perhaps it is an inborn family awareness of mankind's original oneness which partly drives us still to desire the practical unity of the peoples of the world.

Secondly, the Bible tells us that the greatest obstacle to world peace and unity is not simply in the realm of ideas and differing religious or political opinions. The impression is often given that the blocks to unity are only in our minds. If only people were to give up their creeds, or relax their principles, then all would be well. But this assumption behind the modern drive for religious pluralism is far too simplistic. This is plain from the fact that even people who have the same religious creed or political ideals still often manage to fall out with each other. History is littered with movements which have fragmented into splinter groups which differ hardly at all in their basic outlook. Another factor is subtly at work in these divisions.

The greatest obstacle to human unity is in fact what we popularly call human nature. One of the most endearing and yet at the same time disappointing features of mankind is that wherever you go in the world human nature is basically the same. Once we have got past the superficial differences of culture and language, we recognize that other folk are pretty much like ourselves. We are all vulnerable; we all have needs for human love and joy. There is good and bad in everyone. The good endears people to us. The bad disappoints and perhaps even frightens us. There is good, the Bible would tell us, because each person is precious, originally made in the image of God. There is bad because human nature has been perverted from its original state and has a darker side. The Bible relates the rebellion of the first male and female against God in the garden of Eden as a moral rebellion, which has now been translated into the hearts of us all. There is a self-centredness and independence, a hardness of heart, which infects all the human family. Psychologists tell us that very often these dark forces operate in the realm of the unconscious and are not part of our conscious intentions or beliefs. To say that the divisions in mankind are fundamentally about creeds and ideas is too shallow. The Bible speaks of the sinful heart. Across the world social problems and law and order problems may vary in extent but they do not vary in kind. The same old vices of greed and indifference, lies and stealing, adultery and hatred, beleaguer every country, every nationality. It is foolish to think that it is only differences of ideas and ideals which cause trouble and division within mankind.

The fundamental obstacles to unity and love between the people of the world are moral. The problem is fallen human nature. The history of the world is to a large extent a catalogue of man's inhumanity to man. We may call it selfishness or pride; the Bible calls it sin. Sin isolates and separates. And it is sin which not only separates God and man, but also separates people. Moral rebellion has not only ruined mankind's relationship with God, but it ruins our relationship with one another. James, the brother of Jesus, writes in the New Testament, 'What causes fights and quarrels among you? Don't they come from your desires that battle within you? You want something but don't get it. You kill and covet, but you cannot have what you want. You quarrel and fight' (James 4:1-2). That is realism. The deduction to be made from all this is that because the problem which bedevils the quest for unity among people is precisely the same as that which separates man from God it is not possible to solve one problem without the other. In particular, secure and lasting reconciliation between people can be achieved only as human nature is changed and as they are reconciled to God. It is only as the human heart is changed that society can really be changed for the good.

This consideration cuts both ways. It speaks to the world and to the church. It tells the world that although its search for reconciliation between people is fine and noble, this cannot be achieved apart from God. It tells the church, as Jesus did, that any belligerent, bombastic promotion of Christianity which does not include a deep respect and love for all people and a desire for 'peace on earth' is false. This is Christianity's perception of the root problem.

Thirdly, what we have touched on leads us to an initial answer to the criticisms of Christ as the only way. In brief, the Bible's insistence on one way of salvation does not spring from any narrow-mindedness or narrow-heartedness in God, but from the fundamental unity of mankind. Because human nature is the same in us all, because the problem of sin is the same for us all, the remedy must be the same for us all. It is because Christianity sees the differences between East and West, black and white, male and female, educated and

# One way

uneducated, rich and poor, as ultimately not fundamental differences, that it preaches one way of salvation. It is for this reason that Jesus is set forth as 'the Saviour of the world' (John 4:42). It is for this reason that Jesus is able to declare, 'If *anyone* is thirsty, let him come to me and drink. *Whoever* believes in me, as the Scripture has said, streams of living water will flow from within him' (John 7:37). Because people are essentially the same, they require the same remedy.

We may also say that by contrast the pluralist view, that 'Religion is a purely private matter and each of us must be left to find his or her own way', is in fact to say that people and their basic needs are fundamentally different. We all need a different way of salvation because we are so diverse. It therefore implies that mankind is not a true family and that the search for oneness is an impossible task.

Having made these initial remarks, which set out the essence of the rationale behind Christianity's insistence on one way of salvation, we proceed next to look in greater detail at three major areas of biblical teaching pertaining to this matter. The three areas are those of revelation, redemption and regeneration.

## 1. Revelation

Sin has severed the original links of communication between God and man. Adam and Eve were shut out of the garden of God's presence. How then are we to discover the truth about God and his ways? The term 'revelation' comes from the word 'reveal' and speaks of how God reveals himself to mankind, how he makes himself known.

Notice that we have spoken of revelation as the activity of God. God is the agent, not man. God makes himself known to us. We cannot find him without his help.

In the quest for learning mankind is endowed with the great

faculty of reason. Our minds are indeed tools of enormous power in gaining understanding and we like to work things out for ourselves and not be dependent on others. Superficially it may appear that reason and revelation are somehow opposites. But this is to misunderstand both the nature and limitations of autonomous reason.

An example will help to elucidate this. Not long ago I was speaking at a college of law in the south of England on the subject of how God may be known. In order to show the limitations of independent reasoning and the necessity of revelation, I asked the students what they knew about the architect of the college buildings. This simple question leads us to two lessons about reason.

## The limitations of reason

Knowing that students are proverbially bad at reading college handbooks, I asked if anyone present knew the *name* of the architect who had designed the college buildings. No one seemed to know. I suggested that we try an experiment. Suppose, say, six of the students tried over the next few days to reason out the answer to the question of the identity of the architect just by looking at the buildings, could any of them do it? Could it be done by pure deduction, without having the information 'revealed' to them by looking into the college handbook? The general opinion was 'no', it could not be done. Again, if the six did each manage to come to some conclusion as to the architect's identity, what would be the likelihood of their all agreeing as to the answer? Again the general consensus was that the likelihood of their agreeing would be exceedingly small and even if more than one did arrive at the same conclusion, their agreement would be no indication that they had reached the right answer.

Now the point here is that as human beings we sit on our planet in this vast universe and we feel drawn to think of what

# One way

life is all about and about the Maker of this great place and try to come to some conclusions about God using our minds. That is an understandable exercise. But if we concluded that it would hardly be possible, using nothing but our deductive powers, to come to a definite conclusion concerning the architect of the law college, how much less chance have we of coming to a correct conclusion about God? And surely all the plethora of differing ideas in the world about God and religion points to that fact. The Hindu would say that there are many gods. Judaism and Islam point to one God. Buddhism and Western scientific materialism would say there is no God. That seems to cover all the options! We have a total conflict of views. There are no doubt sincere and thoughtful people in all the faiths, but left to ourselves and our reason, we are just not capable of coming to a certain answer.

If we are going to know the answer to the question concerning who is the architect of the college, we are dependent on information being given to us. It needs to be revealed to us, perhaps through the college handbook or by someone who was around when the college was built. Just so, the Christian would say, the idea that independent reason can lead us to certainty about God (or indeed certainty about anything) is pure fancy. Reason is always dependent on, and limited by, the quality of the initial information from which it starts.

## The attitude of reason

If we wanted or needed to know not just the architect's identity, but what sort of person he is and what he thinks, we should need to go a stage further in our assessment of reason. Imagine that the architect was now standing before us and that we wished to find out what he was thinking. We could approach him either as an object or as a person.

We could treat him as an object, such that trust does not enter into our relationship. Here we, the investigators, are in control. We could set out trying to analyse the architect's character, but we would not get far unless he co-operated. We could try to force him to answer questions by administering truth drugs, but in administering the drugs we would be changing his mental state; we would not know him as he really was. We could perform operations to dissect his brain and find out how it worked, but, of course, by doing so we would kill him. We could set about an unlimited number of such experiments, but treating the architect as an object will never help us to know him and his character.

But if, by contrast, we did not treat him as an object but as a person, a whole area of previously unavailable knowledge would be opened up to us. If we trust someone as a free subject, listen to the answers to the questions we put to him, answer the questions he puts to us, and allow ourselves to enter a relationship with him, things which before were totally inaccessible then become open to us. Once we have moved from an attitude of distrust to one of trust, real communication is possible. And it is plain that in moving from the first attitude to the second, what has happened is not that we have rejected the use of reason. We are still rational people making rational judgements. The difference is that now reason is playing a different role. Reason has become a listener rather than a master and we can only know other people by becoming trustful listeners.

Like the architect in our illustration, God is not an object, he is a person. We can never find out the truth about God and how he thinks by adopting an independent, detached view of him. If we want to know, we must have the attitude of trusting listeners. Having listened, it may then be right and proper for us to check what we have learned against our knowledge of life and of the world in general, but we can never know God unless God speaks and we are prepared to listen. But it is exactly at this point that the problem of human sin rears its head. Sin is rebellion against God. The essence of sin is a spirit which refuses to listen. Nevertheless, Christianity claims, God has sought to reveal himself to us.

If we wanted to know not just the architect's identity, but what sort of person he is and, say, what he thinks of the college now, it would be best for him to come and tell us in person and for us to listen. We can never deduce another person's thoughts. We can only find out what they are if he or she reveals them to us. Similarly, if we are going to know with certainty about God and his ways, there is only one way: it is for him to come and tell us. This, of course, is the great claim concerning Jesus, the Son of God: 'In the beginning was the Word, and the Word was with God, and the Word was God. The Word became flesh and made his dwelling among us. We have seen his glory, the glory of the One and Only, who came from the Father, full of grace and truth' (John 1:1,14).

One of the wise men of the Old Testament, Agur son of Jakeh, realized the hopelessness of trying to find God by his own wisdom. He declared:

'I am the most ignorant of men;
    I do not have a man's understanding.
I have not learned wisdom,
    nor have I knowledge of the Holy One.
Who has gone up to heaven and come down?...
What is his name and the name of his son?
    Tell me if you know'

(Proverbs 30:2-4).

This must be the conclusion of every right-minded man, no matter how wise. To pretend to know about God, to pretend to be certain of either his existence or non-existence, purely on the basis of our own autonomous reason and wisdom, is sheer arrogance. The great twentieth-century philosopher Ludwig Wittgenstein declared in his *Tractatus Logico-Philosophius*, 'Whereof one cannot speak, thereof one must be silent.' Agur, son of Jakeh, had reached a similar conclusion many years before. No one can speak with certainty of the things of God and heaven except one who has ascended to heaven and come back to reveal to us what he has found.

But speaking one night to another wise religious man, Nicodemus, Jesus gave the answer to Agur's problem. He said, 'I have spoken to you of earthly things and you do not believe; how then will you believe if I speak of heavenly things? No one has ever gone into heaven except the one who came from heaven — the Son of Man' (John 3:13). The 'Son of Man' was one of Jesus' favourite ways of speaking of himself. By saying this Jesus was claiming to be the one sent from heaven to reveal to us what we could never reason out for ourselves. He claimed to be the Son of God, equal with the Father, sent from the Father's side to reveal God and his ways to us. To his disciple Philip he said, 'Anyone who has seen me has seen the Father' (John 14:9). There were many religions and many religious teachers in Jesus' day, just as there have been down the centuries, saying, 'I think this or that about God.' But actually it is very arrogant and foolish for any of us to declare what is true or not true concerning God purely on the basis of our own reason. There is need for revelation and Jesus claims that he is the true revelation, the perfect embodiment of all that is true about God.

As yet we have not considered the credibility of Jesus' claims, but we can see why it is that Christianity proclaims Christ as the only way. Mankind needs revelation. There is one way of salvation because there is one God, and no other, and he has come in the person of Jesus Christ to reveal the truth concerning himself.

Before we proceed any further a couple of points could be made. The Christian is often branded as arrogant because he has firm convictions concerning God. (Let me say again that Christians should never have an arrogant attitude.) But logically I would suggest that it is the militant agnostics or atheists who are actually the arrogant ones. The militant agnostic is telling us that he or she is uncertain about God. Fine. But then if such people go on to say that we too must be uncertain and have no right to be firm in our convictions, on what basis are they saying that? If they are uncertain, how can they be certain that we are not right? And if they are not sure of this why do they insist that the Christian must *not* be firm in his convictions? It would seem to be on the basis that 'If I am not certain of my position, it is wrong for you to be certain of yours,' which is surely pure arrogance, simply telling people, 'You must think as I do'!

The militant atheist is in the same position. If the philosophers are correct and it is impossible to come to certainty concerning things by means of pure deduction, nevertheless the atheist has come to be certain, so he thinks, that there is no God. Very well, but how has he come to this conclusion? Nothing has been revealed to him, for according to him there is no God to reveal anything. He has come to his conclusion purely on his own ability to reason, he must say. Thus the source of his certainty is in himself alone. Although all the philosophers say we cannot reason it out — he has. Here is arrogance.

The Christian is in a different position. He has come to be sure concerning God. But having come to certainty, the Christian has no cause to be proud, rather the opposite. For the Christian's certainty is not based on himself and his own deductive processes, but only on what God has chosen to reveal concerning Jesus. The Christian has no room to boast. Once again we see that humility is therefore the only fitting attitude for Christian witness.

## 2. Redemption

Not only do people need to *know about* God, as one knows about facts; they need to *know* him, as one knows another person. The broken relationship between God and mankind needs to be re-established. How can we have living contact with God?

By way of understanding why Christianity is proclaiming Christ as the only way of salvation, we need to understand that Christianity tells us, as we have already noted, that the problem which separates God and man is a moral one. It is the problem of human sin before the pure and holy God.

There is a darker side to human nature, which not only lies at the root of the failure of all human relationships (family break-up, lies, theft, personal selfishness, violence in society, etc.), but which has ruined our relationship with God. People are cut off from God through sin.

The idea of sin is very unfashionable nowadays, but it is a reality. Few people will acknowledge this twisted side of human nature, but just sometimes people will be honest with themselves. For example, in 1986 a bill was introduced in Parliament to ban nude pin-ups in newspapers, but was derided and thrown out of the House of Commons. Not long after that, a well-known woman journalist, who had always in the past argued against censorship and for freedom of expression, wrote in one of the national magazines the following: 'Do you know, as one of those liberals who has spent many words expressing just such views, I find myself thinking now, "I do not care any more"? Such a great fight for what we called freedom and what do we end up with? ... children allowed to watch sex and video nasties by parents who should know better; women's bodies used to sell everything; men so sated with sexual "freedom" that they purchase little children as they used to do in the 19th century. As a good liberal you spend your life saying, "Oh, it won't do any harm", and "Live and let live" — until one morning you wake up and look out on a world which is a considerably nastier place than the one your parents knew when you were a child. Perhaps you cannot prove it nastier; but in your heart you *know*. And perhaps feel somewhat responsible.'[1]

Here is someone with rare honesty and what is being said is, at the very least, that when human nature is let off the leash, when 'freedom of expression' reigns, the world becomes a nastier place. She is right. Sin is a reality.

In the Gulf War of 1991 when the coalition forces eventually retook Kuwait City, the extent of the Iraqi atrocities against the people of the capital came to light. The allied commander General Norman Schwarzkopf said of those who had committed the atrocities, 'I just have to pray that those people are of a different race from us!' Now that was a 'knee-jerk' remark in response to the horror of what had happened, but obviously the perpetrators of those crimes are not of another race. They are of the human race. These terrible things are just an extreme example of what human nature is capable of. There is something twisted and corrupt in human nature which makes man's inhumanity to man only too possible. This is the presence of sin, and it is sin which forms the moral gulf which separates people from people and people from God.

It is worth saying that the reality of sin should give the Christian every cause for humility rather than arrogance. A Christian is someone who has come to be convicted of his or her sin in the sight of God and to see himself or herself as in need of redemption. To think of ourselves as in some way better than others or above others should be far from the Christian. How can a person who has come to realize the depth of inconsistency and corruption in his own character be proud?

A consideration of the nature of sin, based on Scripture, will lead us to see yet another reason why Christianity insists on the one sole way of salvation in Christ. There are two things to say.

First, because since mankind's first rebellion against God, sin is endemic in us, *we cannot redeem or rescue ourselves from it*. Salvation can never be by way of self-help. The Bible emphasizes this in a series of rhetorical questions which all require a negative reply:

'Who can bring what is pure from the impure?'
>    (Job 14:4).

'Can the Ethiopian change his skin
>    or the leopard its spots?
> Neither can you do good
>    who are accustomed to doing evil!'
>    (Jeremiah 13:23).

'With what shall I come before the Lord
>    and bow down before the exalted God?...
> Will the Lord be pleased with thousands of rams,
>    with ten thousand rivers of oil?
> Shall I offer my firstborn for my transgression,
>    the fruit of my body for the sin of my soul?'
>    (Micah 6:6-7).

No, there is no ritual of personal cleansing, no act of self-reformation, no extremity of personal sacrifice which is capable of making amends for sin in the sight of God. The idea of self-redemption is as ineffectual and as ludicrous as for a man to attempt to pull himself up by his own bootstraps. It is as impossible as a dirty child making himself clean by means of his own grubby hands.

Furthermore, not only is such a scheme of religion impossible, it would also be obnoxious, for those who felt they had done enough to save themselves would have reason to boast over those who had not. Such religion would be a breeding ground for Pharisaism and self-congratulation.

Secondly, this matter of human sin is in fact of such gigantic moment, says the Bible, that not only are we totally unable to redeem ourselves, but *even God himself was shut in to only one possible way of saving us*, and that a most difficult way.

Sin presented God with an enormous problem. He is a God of love, but at the same time he is the God of justice. As the

Lawgiver and Judge of mankind, he has to be, in fact, the very benchmark of impartiality and jurisprudence. Sin is moral failure, and just as when the laws of our land are broken we look for justice to be done, so justice has to be done for sin. If a police-officer is found to be corrupt, or a judge fails to carry out the law impartially, turning a blind eye, or accepting a bribe, we are rightly outraged. If a government minister uses his or her influence unfairly to benefit particular friends it rightly provokes public fury. We expect integrity in those in authority. We properly insist on the rule of law being upheld. God is holy and, for all his love to mankind, could not let the guilt of sin pass. The Judge of all the earth must do that which is right. He must maintain his integrity. For him to remain a just Judge, the punishment due to sin must be meted out. And yet if that happens how could men and women be saved from condemnation? There was only one way for his moral integrity to be kept intact and at the same time for sinners to be saved. This could only be accomplished by his coming himself to pay sin's penalty. God had to come in the person of his Son, Jesus. Jesus had to go to the cross bearing the sin of the world. He would clear our moral debt in the eyes of justice. There was no other way.

That the cross was the only possible way is surely borne out by two particular incidents in the Gospel accounts of Christ's life.

The first is at Cæsarea Philippi, where came the first declaration from the disciples that they recognized who Jesus really was. In reply to the question from Jesus, 'Who do you say I am?', Simon Peter answered, 'You are the Christ, the Son of the living God' (Matthew 16:15,16). Soon after that we read, 'From that time on Jesus began to explain to his disciples that he must go to Jerusalem and suffer many things at the hands of the elders, chief priests and teachers of the law, and that he must be killed and on the third day be raised to life.' Having identified who he really was, Jesus felt able to begin to explain to his disciples his mission, which would take him to his death. At this, out of love and care for his Master, we read, 'Peter took him aside and began to rebuke him. "Never, Lord!" he said. "This shall never happen to you!" Jesus turned and said to Peter, "Get behind me, Satan! You are a stumbling-block to me; you do not have in mind the things of God, but the things of men"' (Matthew 16:21-23).

The force of Jesus' reply makes it clear to us that the cross was an absolute necessity. He could not afford to listen. Peter was speaking out of loving concern for his friend Jesus. He desired to shield him from such a destiny. But even the loving concern of a devoted disciple, who would divert him from the road to Calvary, had to be rebuked. Christ's death was the only way that his mission could be completed and sinners saved.

The second incident, which spells this out in even more graphic detail, is the prayer of Jesus in the Garden of Gethsemane. It was the night before he was crucified. As the soldiers were coming to arrest him, Jesus was in the garden in prayer. There, it would seem, the full extent of what it would mean for him to bear our sins was revealed to Jesus as never before. He felt nearly overwhelmed with the horror of it. The Gospel writer Luke records for us that such was Jesus' anguish that his sweat was like drops of blood falling to the ground. Here we see just how serious a matter sin really is. If anyone has the idea that sin can be dealt with easily, go to Gethsemane. Christ is God become man. We say it reverently, but such is the seriousness of sin that, as the full realization of what was entailed in atoning for sin weighed upon him, it caused God himself to tremble. Jesus was in an agony of anguish. So it was that he prayed, 'My Father, if it is possible, may this cup be taken from me. Yet not as I will, but as you will' (Matthew 26:39). Here is the Son pleading with his Father in heaven, who loved him infinitely, that if there was some other way in which God's plan could be accomplished and sinners saved, he might be excused the appalling suffering which awaited him at

Calvary. But there was no other way. The only reply his Father could give to Jesus was to strengthen him for the coming task. Jesus must be crucified for our sin.

Now perhaps we can see that Jesus' words, 'No one comes to the Father except through me,' are not the words of some overbearing megalomaniac. They are the sober, kindly words of the Son of God who loved us and gave himself for us, and who knew the seriousness of sin and what it would cost him to save us. Sin is so serious that no one else could open the way to God. No mere man could lift sin's weight. No angel in heaven could carry sin's burden. Only the death of the Son of God himself could make atonement. Humbly and worshipfully we realize why there is only one way for God to save us.

## Regeneration

The word 'regeneration' refers to individuals being remade as people. It means being reborn.

Not only must our ignorance of God, which is the result of sin, be dispelled by Christ's revelation and the guilt of sin be dealt with by Christ's redemption, but sin's power in our lives must be broken if human nature is really to change and people are to begin to lead at a personal level something approaching the lives of love and justice which our world needs. There must be personal spiritual rebirth.

The following quotation is worth considering: 'No other of the great religions offers this atoning sacrifice of the incarnate God. All the rest appear to think that the condition of sincere repentance and amendment is enough... It might be so if sin were merely a kind of error which could be retrieved by second thoughts, or a passing infection which our essentially healthy constitution could throw off. It is thus that most of the great religions regard it, they dare not do otherwise, or they would find the problem insoluble. But Christianity takes a graver view... For our deliverance we need the injection into our lives of a new power, a power not native to us but capable of remaking us, a power which Christ alone can and did supply; and he supplied it by his passion and death.'[2]

Christianity offers a new power for our lives: a power which will not make us immediately perfect, but will enable us to make progress in living as God would have us live, in love and dignity. This power is the power of Christ's Holy Spirit, who comes into our lives to regenerate us as people.

There is only one person who has lived a human life as it should be lived. That is Jesus. He alone lived a life 'full of grace and truth'. He alone has lived without sin, fully obeying all God's commands from the heart. His obedience to God the Father extended even to his death on the cross in order to accomplish God's plan of redemption for mankind.

Through his death on the cross Christ has made it possible for his own Spirit to be released into the lives of ordinary men and women like ourselves. His is the Spirit of truth and love and lowly, joyful obedience to God. After his death, Christ was raised on the third day and later ascended into heaven; from there he poured out his Spirit upon the church on the Day of Pentecost. The powerful Spirit of him who has already pleased God in every way is made available to change us and to aid us in living our lives.

Only Jesus has lived so as fully to please the Father. This wonderful Holy Spirit, who enables us to imitate Christ and to please God in daily living, is available from no other source. He is the Spirit of Jesus. Thus, as we understand this further aspect of the Bible's teaching concerning salvation, we understand once again why there is the insistence on there being only one way, and that way being Christ.

Jesus said, 'I am the way and the truth and the life. No one comes to the Father except through me.' Now we can see the reasons for Christ's claim. Only he could reveal the Father to us — for he alone (with the Holy Spirit) is one with the Father.

*One way*

Only he could deal with the problem of man's moral failure, for he alone could make atonement for sin. Only he has lived so as fully to please God and he alone could share with us his Spirit to enable us to begin to live as God intends. So it is that the Lord Jesus claimed to be the only way to God.

# 4.
# Why only Jesus?

Why should we accept the claims of Jesus to be the only way to God? What is the evidence? Obviously a great deal could be said on this question and here I can only state briefly some of the factors which weigh with me personally. However, before I come to those, one thing I want to say is that if the reader is not a Christian and is unfamiliar with the Bible narrative, it would be very good for you to read something of the Bible yourself, especially one of the Gospels. Sadly, very often people seem to make up their minds concerning Jesus without having given due consideration to what we know of him. Preconceived ideas help nobody. I would encourage you to look at what is recorded of the life of Jesus in the Gospels so that you can come to your own conclusion in a considered way.

Speaking personally, there are four matters which lead me to believe that the claims of Jesus are true. They are the coming of Jesus, the character of Jesus, the resurrection of Jesus and the message of Jesus. We will consider each one of these briefly.

## 1. The coming of Jesus

The Old Testament paved the way for the coming of Jesus. The Old Testament was complete and standardized at least 200

# Why only Jesus?

years before Jesus' birth and yet it is full of predictions which exactly fit his life. On the following page you will find a table which summarizes just some of the Old Testament prophecies concerning Jesus and how they were apparently fulfilled. I would encourage you to check these for yourself and ask yourself, how could these things happen?

Of course it could be said that Jesus, knowing the predictions concerning the Christ, deliberately sought to fulfil the Old Testament Scriptures. That is certainly true concerning some of the references: for example, John tells us concerning the crucifixion, 'Later, knowing that all was now completed, and so that the Scripture would be fulfilled, Jesus said, "I am thirsty"' (John 19:28). So he did deliberately seek to fulfil some prophecies. However, that cannot be true for all the prophecies. No ordinary person could deliberately fulfil the prophecies concerning the miracles, or indeed the time and place of his birth. 'When evening came, many who were demon-possessed were brought to him, and he drove out the spirits with a word and healed all the sick. This was to fulfil what was spoken through the prophet Isaiah: "He took up our infirmities and carried our diseases"' (Matthew 8:16-17). Think these matters through. The evidence is before you. Check through the table of prophecies for yourself. Doesn't it indeed point to the absolute uniqueness of Jesus?

## 2. The character of Jesus

Reading the Gospels, we come into close acquaintance with the character of Jesus. For myself, as I consider Jesus' character, it is indeed the kind of character which fits with his claim to be God become man. For example, he made the great claim to be the way, the truth and the life, the only way to the Father. But there was evidently no mania or obsession attached to these claims. He was not a person in search of acclaim or power

| Old Testament reference | Approximate date of writing | Summary | New Testament fulfilment | Comment |
| --- | --- | --- | --- | --- |
| Genesis 12:3 | 1500 B.C. | The Jews would be the means of God's blessing to all nations. | Matthew 1:1 | Jesus Christ, God's Saviour, was a Jew. |
| Genesis 49:10 | 1500 B.C. | The Christ would come from the Jewish tribe of Judah. | Matthew 1:3 | Both Mary and Joseph, Jesus' parents, were from the tribe of Judah — in fact from the line of King David. |
| Micah 5:2 | 700 B.C. | The Christ would be born in Bethlehem. | Luke 2: 4-7 | Jesus was born in Bethlehem. |
| Isaiah 61:1-3; 11:1-5 | 700 B.C. | The Christ would inaugurate God's kingdom of peace, healing and salvation. | Luke 4:17-19 | Not even Jesus' enemies could deny the miracles of healing which Jesus so obviously performed. |
| Daniel 2:1-47 | 580 B.C. | God's kingdom would be set up during the time of the fourth empire to dominate the Middle East starting from the time of Nebuchadnezzar. | Mark 1:15 | The four empires are identified as: first Babylon; second Medes, that is Persia; third Greece; fourth Rome. Jesus lived and declared the kingdom in the time of Roman domination of Palestine. |
| Isaiah 53<br>Psalm 22:8,16 | 700 B.C.<br>1000 B.C. | God's Christ would suffer and die for our sins. | Luke 23:22-33 | Christ was crucified along with two criminals while people mocked him. |
| Isaiah 53:11<br>Psalm 16:10 | 700 B.C.<br>1000 B.C. | The Christ would rise from the dead. | Acts 2:22-33 | The tomb of Jesus was empty and the first disciples were sure. |
| Isaiah 42:6; 49:6 | 700 B.C. | The Christ would bring salvation to both Jews and Gentiles. | Matthew 28:19-20<br>Revelation 7:9-10 | The Christian gospel continues to spread through the world today, bringing salvation to all who believe, and so God's promise to Abraham, that through his descendants all nations would be blessed, is even now being fulfilled. |

# Why only Jesus?

over others. At one point in the story, having seen his miracles, the people wanted to make Jesus their king. His reaction was to go away and hide himself (John 6:15). He very often charged those he healed not to broadcast what he had done for them (Mark 1:44). Palm Sunday, just before his death, was the first time that he let his disciples make public who he really was and even then he rode into Jerusalem not with pomp and majesty, but lowly and astride a donkey.

Jesus is very meek and yet at the same time very disturbing. Once the disciples were afraid when they were caught in a great storm on the Sea of Galilee, but after he had performed the miracle of calming the storm, they were more fearful of Jesus than they had been of the tempest (Mark 4:41). Jesus is also very disturbing in the way he sees right through people and discerns their motives. How unnerving it must have been for the woman of Samaria, whom he met at the well, to realize that Jesus knew all her past, all about her five failed marriages and her yearning for love! Yet at the same time as being powerfully discerning and awesomely authoritative, Christ is infinitely compassionate, sympathetic and kind to people. Very often he was moved to tears over the plight of ordinary people and spent himself to the point of exhaustion in seeking to teach them and help them.

The amazing blend in Christ's personality speaks to me of the character of God. It is the kind of character I would expect of the Alm.ghty — terrifying, and yet exciting and lovely!

## 3. The resurrection of Jesus

Polite society, even today, would not look upon Jesus as a 'nice' person. Patiently and calmly he made what seem to be the most outrageous and egocentric claims for himself. He claimed to have authority to forgive people their sins (Mark 2:10). He claimed to be the Son of God, indeed God become man (Matthew 26:63-64; John 5:18). He claimed to be the ultimate Judge of the world (John 5:22-23). He claimed, as we have seen, to be the only way to God (John 14:6). Such things are not the kind of things that 'nice' people say. They are stupendous. The religious leaders of Jesus' day had given the thumbs down on Christ. They felt he was a mad fanatic. They called his bluff, as they thought. With the help of the Roman authorities they did away with him. He was put to death by crucifixion. The disciples of Jesus were devastated. Frightened, alarmed and confused, they hid themselves.

But three days later, according to the New Testament story, death could no longer hold him. God raised him from the dead. And the historical evidence for the resurrection of Jesus still stands firm and secure after nearly 2,000 years of scrutiny. People have tried and tried again to explain it away but have failed. The disciples met the risen Christ and were transformed. Unafraid, they went out to proclaim the good news of salvation in Christ to the world.

Jesus claimed to be the Son of God. The Jewish leaders and the Romans said 'No!' and crucified him. But God said 'Yes!' He raised Jesus from the dead and so supernaturally reversed their verdict and vindicated the claims of Christ. Paul writes of Jesus, 'Who though the Spirit of holiness was declared with power to be the Son of God, by his resurrection from the dead' (Romans 1:4).

What is the significance of this? We live in a world of many competing religions and rival philosophies. Which one is true? Many people despair of ever sorting it out. Some suggest that there is no final truth, so it does not ultimately matter which one you follow; a person should just choose whichever philosophy of life he or she feels comfortable with.

But the resurrection cuts right through that. By the resurrection God is lifting up Jesus in the eyes of everyone and declaring, 'This is my Son; here is the truth!' Christianity, it seems, is not just one religion among many. The resurrection sets it apart as *the truth*.

## 4. The message of Jesus

Christ's message is the message of love. His death upon the cross for our sins is the great demonstration of the love of God to mankind. Why do I believe that Christ is the way to God? Putting it simply, because this message of God's love seems to me to be so completely suited to the deepest needs of the human heart, it *has* to be the right way.

Certain questions perpetually arise in the minds of every generation: 'What is the purpose of life?' 'What are the world's greatest needs?' I think for all of us, in our most sane and thoughtful moments, there is not much doubt as to the answer to those questions. The answer is love. There are so many broken and disappointed people, so many empty and lonely people in the world and what they need is love. They need to be made to feel worthwhile, that someone cares. There are so many poor people and sick people in the world. What they need is practical love and care from those with the wherewithal to help. To use life to love, to honestly seek good for other people — that is the purpose of life. For people to love one another — that is the greatest need of the world. Such sentiments fuel the drive towards the vision of one world and are almost universally acknowledged.

But how? How are people to find the strength to love and the will to love? In particular, how can we find the strength to love others when they do not treat us well? It is one thing to speak of the concept of the human family caring for one another as an ideal. But the real world is far from ideal. In the real world often the people we love end up hurting us. People we try to help can cheat us, take us for a ride and misuse us. How can we find the will and the energy to carry on loving in these circumstances? Anyone can love their friends, but how do we manage to love our enemies and those who mistreat us? That is the crucial question at the practical level if we are really serious about love in our world.

It seems to me that only the gospel of Christ can provide an answer here. In the face of the real world we can only find the power to love by knowing that we ourselves are loved by God. The knowledge of the unconditional personal love of God in Christ, taking away our sins and giving us eternal life, is the essential ingredient. It is only here that we can find the strength and security to move towards others seeking their highest good, knowing that we might well be hurt badly by them along the way. It is only Christianity and the cross of Christ which can make sense of that kind of love.

If there is no God, then such love makes no sense for, in the words of Victor Hugo, the conclusion of atheism is 'There is no good, no evil, but there is vegetation.'[1] If there is no ultimate good or evil then the idea that love is a 'good' thing is nonsense. Without God the only rule of life which makes sense is biological survival. The law of the jungle, the survival of the fittest, alone makes sense — not love and certainly not a love which is prepared to be hurt for the good of others.

Again if the only God that exists is a distant, relatively uninterested God, who never came to earth to get alongside mankind in its misery, then why should we not be distant and uninterested towards others? Again if ultimate reality is a multiplicity of gods standing for opposite ideals — the god of love, the god of hate, the god of war, the god of peace — then since no one of these is supreme, there can be no supreme purpose in life.

But if, and only if, the truth behind the universe is a God of profound love, a God who loved us so much as to come and to give himself to death on a cross in rescuing us from our sins, then, and only then, does the ideal of love make sense. And love must make sense if it is to be our *purpose* in life, for the idea of *purpose* presupposes things making sense. When we love, and in particular when we are prepared to take the hurts others may inflict on us and continue to love them, then we are in tune with the very way things really ought to be, for we are in tune with God — the God who is love.

## Why only Jesus?

The greatest need of the world is for people to love one another. But it is only in Christ that we can find the strength to love in the real world and it is only in Christ that such love makes sense.

Christianity does not intend to be arrogant or overbearing, but here is something of the case. Here is a little of the answer as to why the claims of Jesus to be the only way should be accepted.

The Old Testament prophecies reach over such a large period of time that they have the hallmark of God on them and they point very clearly to Jesus as God's Saviour for the world. The character of Jesus, in all its awesome loveliness, indicates his deity. The resurrection of Jesus sets him apart from all others as the man appointed by God as our Redeemer. The message of God's love which Jesus brought speaks so precisely to the needs of the world that he has to be taken seriously in all that he claims.

'I am the way and the truth and the life. No one comes to the Father except through me.' This is the claim of Jesus, and his promise is, 'Whoever comes to me I will never drive away' (John 6:37).

# 5.
# Jesus and other religions

The story of several blind men and the elephant is often told in the interests of religious agnosticism. The story, you remember, is that of a king who brings an elephant to the blind men and asks them to feel the animal with their hands and describe what they think it is like. Because they stand at different positions with respect to the elephant, they touch different areas of the animal's body and so feel different things and begin to argue over the nature of the beast. The king, who is not blind, then explains the situation, tells them they have all got it wrong, and so charges all the blind men to learn in humility from one another, in order that they might come to the truth. This, we are told, is a precise analogy of the confusion and conflict between different religions and their differing views of God. We are all in touch with religious reality, we are told, but because we are blind and approach it from different points of view we come to different conclusions. We should not think we have *the* truth. We should learn from each other.

This all sounds very reasonable and plausible. It is an approach to religion that finds wide acceptance in the world today. However, we have to acknowledge that quite clearly Jesus rejected this view. Humbly, yet firmly, he insisted that 'No one comes to the Father except through me.' Salvation according to Jesus was found only through conscious faith in himself as Lord and Saviour.

# Jesus and other religions

So in this chapter we will be looking briefly at other religions and the biblical assessment of them. In defending Christianity we shall have to say some negative things about other faiths and ideologies. Because criticism of other religions is often identified as 'intolerance', which raises the spectre of persecution, it must be made clear once again here that Christ was completely opposed to religious persecution, and indeed to any compulsion in religious matters. All people should respect one another and learn to live together. But that does not mean that the Christian must agree with others and keep silent concerning Christianity's stress upon Christ as the only way.

## We cannot all be right

The story of the blind men and the elephant at first looks like the ideal solution to the matter of differences of religious conviction. In fact, as we shall see later, it actually reveals enormous arrogance and bases its argument on a grave fallacy which makes it totally unworkable. However, for the moment let us acknowledge that superficially it seems very appealing. It holds out the possibility of saying to all people, 'Well, in a way you are all right! You all have something of the truth.' It therefore seems to provide a convivial and convenient way forward as it tries to please everybody. But if the honest seeker after truth does set out seriously to follow this road he or she quickly runs into trouble. Soon we find our path blocked by insurmountable obstacles. As we view the different ideas embodied in the different faiths, we quickly and sadly see that their views disagree so deeply as to be irreconcilable in almost every crucial area. The ear and the leg of an elephant can be explained reasonably as being different parts of the same animal. But the differences between religions in many vital areas are so fundamental as to be only reconcilable by throwing away our reason. If we do that, the search for truth, at least for rational truth, is negated, and so the quest becomes futile.

The different faiths do not profess to have the same *goal*. For Christianity the end in view, to be sought after in Christ, is endless personal fellowship with God in the resurrected state of the new heavens and new earth. 'But in keeping with his promise we are looking forward to a new heaven and a new earth, the home of righteousness' (2 Peter 3:13). By contrast the goal envisaged by the Eastern religions, like Buddhism or Hinduism, is Nirvana, which involves the final extinction of the individual personality. Christianity tells us that *we* will enjoy heaven; the Eastern religions tell us that there will be no such entity as '*we*'! These things are total opposites. It is not possible to make them fit together. Going back to our analogy, it is not possible to make them part of the same elephant.

Again different faiths do not believe in the same *God*. The tribal religions are polytheistic, believing in many gods. Hinduism is at one level polytheistic, but fundamentally pantheistic, proposing that in fact everything is God and God is everything. Buddhism is atheistic. Marxism says there is no such being as God. Faiths like Christian Science seem to reduce God to a mere impersonal spiritual force. Judaism and Islam are both unitarian, believing that God is indivisibly one, whereas Christianity is trinitarian, and proclaims the mystery of the person of God as being both one and three — Father, Son and Holy Spirit, but one God. Reviewing all these different ideas, we see that they are not just superficially incongruent with each other, but fundamentally opposed. It is no good pretending that they can be reconciled. Rather, without being harsh to others, we have to think through in all honesty which view is correct, which view makes the most sense of the world, and come to a decision.

The examples of the essential disagreements between religions and ideologies can be multiplied. Eastern religions teach reincarnation, that a person dies but then comes back to live in

# Jesus and other religions 51

this world in another form until death comes again. Thus on this view we live and die many times. But the Bible says, 'Man is destined to die *once* and after that to face judgement' (Hebrews 9:27). Again Islam has much to say about Jesus, but declares that it was not Jesus who died on the cross; it was someone else. We cannot both be right.

The story of the blind men and the elephant is actually rather shallow and, although attractive at first glance, fails to face the problem seriously. Professor Zaehner, who came from a Hindu background, was for many years professor of Eastern Religions at Oxford. He said this: 'To maintain that all religions are paths leading to the same goal, as is frequently done today, is to maintain something that is not true. Not only on the dogmatic, but also on the mystical plane too, there is no agreement. It is then only too true that the basic principles of Eastern and Western thought are, I will not say irreconcilably opposed, they simply are not starting from the same premises. The only common ground is that the function of religion is to provide release; there is no agreement as to what it is that man must be released from. The great religions are talking at cross purposes.'[1]

Making a harmony out of all religions and ideologies is impossible. Sadly we have to say that it is dishonest to make out that there can be such harmony.

## Some objections to other religions

As we now consider some of the problems with other religions, let me say clearly that we are not to think that everything in other faiths is totally without value. Certainly not. There is often much that is wise. There can be great integrity and high moral standards in other faiths, which the Christian would say are there by the common grace of God. Again, these faiths contain things which are viewed as sacred by many people, and ideas which have brought comfort to many people down the years. We are not to trample roughshod over these things in an uncaring way. But, nevertheless, Christianity has to insist on Jesus alone and the deceptiveness of any 'other gospel'. The apostle Paul puts this in strong language: 'But even if we or an angel from heaven should preach a gospel other than the one we preached to you, let him be eternally condemned! As we have already said, so now I say again: If anybody is preaching to you a gospel other than what you accepted, let him be eternally condemned!' (Galatians 1:8-9).

In assessing other faiths, I can only give my own, perhaps rather limited thinking on this matter. But let me share my personal view.

The place to start is to explain my strategy in all this. I suppose it is a very practical mode of considering ideas. It seems to me that if philosophies and faiths are untrue they will lead in practice to disastrous results for human beings. Conversely, when we find the truth about God, and about ourselves, it will actually bring the greatest good to human beings. All this goes back to some very down-to-earth words of Jesus. He said, 'By their fruit you will recognize them. Do people pick grapes from thornbushes, or figs from thistles? Likewise every good tree bears good fruit, but a bad tree bears bad fruit' (Matthew 7:16-7). That has always seemed to me to make very sound sense.

We shall divide up the current major non-Christian philosophies and faiths of the world, into six categories: atheistic materialism, Eastern religions (Hinduism, Buddhism etc.), Islam, Judaism, Bible cults and the New Age Movement.

Let us think a little about each of these.

## 1. Atheistic materialism

The greatest experiment in consistent atheism that the world has so far seen has been the Marxist revolution and subsequent government of China, Russia and Eastern Europe for the majority of the twentieth century. This is not to say that there is no atheism in the West. Of course there is! But it is not a consistently worked out atheism. Our governments run according to an atheistic ideology, but pragmatically and on a basis which still contains many Christian ideas. In the Eastern bloc countries during the middle years of this century atheism was applied consistently. If there is no God then the things of the spirit are an illusion and ultimately the only meaningful things are material objects. If there is no God, then the only power to whom people owe allegiance is the state, and the state, which seeks to provide for them, has sovereign rights over the people. What has all this brought about in those countries? It has brought unmitigated disaster. The peoples who have lived under such regimes have rejected Communism wherever they could.

A few years ago I was asked to go and speak to a meeting of the local branch of the Labour Party in our town on the subject of the 'social usefulness of religion' and to enter into a debate with someone who would oppose my Christian position and argue for atheistic socialism. It was quite a lively and interesting debate, but the contribution which had the most effect upon the meeting came from neither of us debaters. Strangely, that very week a Christian pastor from Poland was staying in our town. I asked him to attend the meeting with me. This was in the days before the total overthrow of Communism in Poland. Towards the end of the debate the Polish pastor got to his feet and in broken English simply related something of the conditions in Poland at that time: the shortages, the fear, the lack of freedom. The meeting became very silent. He explained that atheistic socialism as an ideal was one thing; in practice it was something very different. The young socialists were somewhat subdued, to say the least.

The story is told that an old woman once went to Mr Gorbachev and asked if it was a politician or a scientist who invented Communism. Mr Gorbachev replied that he did not know, but thought it was a politician. 'Ah, that explains it,' said the old lady, 'If it had been a scientist he would have tried it on mice first!' That sums up how the peoples of Eastern Europe view the years of Communism. They feel they have been the guinea pigs for a grand experiment which has failed.

But what in particular lies behind the failure of the Communist experiment? Those countries focused on education for the people, planning for their countries. They adopted a so-called scientific approach to human life. Their ideals, at least on paper, were meant to be for the good of all the people in their countries. So what went wrong? It is interesting to reflect on the words of Alexander Solzhenitsyn, the novelist who suffered in the labour camps of the USSR. What he has to say reflects not just on Communism, but on the atheistic humanism of the West. In his Harvard Lecture a few years ago he said, 'The tilt of freedom in the direction of evil has come about gradually, but it was evidently born primarily out of a humanistic and benevolent concept according to which there is no evil inherent in human nature.'

It is simply the perversity of human nature which has turned the ideals of Communism into a nightmare and brought those countries to the edge of catastrophe. The ideals of socialism, with each man looking after his brother, are to be applauded. But in practice people cannot live up to their ideals. We are sinners. The rejection of Christianity, and in particular the Christian view of man as a sinner, is similarly bringing a gradual disaster upon the West, too, in the breakdown of law and order. Without God, the only master of society is man himself. But sadly, man does not have the integrity or the selflessness to be such a master. Consistent atheism bears bad fruit and therefore the conclusion is that its root is bad. It is not the truth.

*Eastern religions*

The Eastern religions like Hinduism and Buddhism do not believe that behind the universe there is a person. They do not

# Jesus and other religions

believe in an ultimate personal God. This basic assumption leads on to affect their view of people as individuals. This is best explained by a comparison of these ideas with the Bible's teaching about human beings.

At the beginning of the Bible the creation of the universe is described. In Genesis chapters 1 and 2 reference is made to how God created the first human pair, Eve and Adam. The first human couple were made 'in the image of God' (Genesis 1:26-27), as self-conscious, personal beings. Being made in the image of God is unique to human beings. This is true of nothing else in the visible universe. Thus the human individual is viewed by the Bible as being of extreme value and dignity.

The next chapter of the Bible, Genesis 3, goes on to describe man's initial rebellion, the entry of sin into the world and man's alienation from God. But, amazingly, it then sets the scene for the greatest drama of love conceivable. The message of the Bible goes on to explain how that, despite man's disobedience and sinful corruption, God still loved us and came, in the person of his Son Jesus, to die for our redemption. Here again human worth is spelled out. Despite our sins, God views the individual human being as so precious that he was prepared to come to the cross of Calvary and die for our salvation. Every soul is priceless.

Christianity then goes on to preach love for our fellow man. Thus the carrying of the Christian gospel has often been accompanied in history by works of care and compassion, medicine, relief work, education for people. The gospel speaks to the whole man and would see each one brought to his or her full potential. A man's or woman's personal contribution to society is viewed as unique and irreplaceable.

In Eastern thought, however, the individual is viewed as just a part of the oneness of the universal soul (*atman*). That being the case, the individual is not seen to be greatly important. In fact individuality is looked upon as something to be denigrated and even erased. Such an outlook inevitably tends to the stunting of human personality and human relationships and the improvement of societies. It is interesting to see that all the major advances in learning and science which have led to the development of modern civilization have come about from the base of Western Christendom. Here, especially after the Reformation, Christianity encouraged the individual to explore God's world, and to see himself as God's image, thinking God's thoughts after him. Here the individual, made in the likeness of his Creator, was encouraged to be a creator and an inventor himself. Why was it that the great benefits of technology arose in the West? Was it because Western people are somehow more able, more clever, than those in the East? Certainly not. That would be pure racism. But it seems to me that it was because the Christian faith encouraged individual thought and creativity, whereas the Eastern outlook discouraged it.

Eastern thought tends to be rather indifferent to the individual. The goal of Hinduism is spoken of, for example, in these terms: 'The perfect dawn is near when you will mingle your life with all life.' The British judge, Christmas Humphries, who was a Buddhist, speaks of so-called Nirvana, the final release, like this: 'Through the destruction of all that is individual in us, we enter into communion with the whole universe and become an integral part of the great purpose.'[2] The goal of Eastern religion is a condition in which people cease to think, or to feel as individuals. It is really a condition in which 'I' shall cease to be at all. Now why should anyone hope for, or seek, such a condition, unless he regards his own individual personality as being of no account? Individuality is looked upon as evil. It is this which separates the person from the universal soul. But to denigrate the individual is, it seems to me, essentially inhuman. This leads to the debasing of human life. It must inevitably lead to people viewing themselves as worthless. At such a point, I have to say that this is a wrong road for mankind.

## Islam

With between seven and eight hundred million Muslims in the world, Islam is now the second largest world religion. It is a religion which has its roots in the same soil as Judaism and Christianity, having arisen in the Middle East and even acknowledging the Bible to a certain extent. However, Islam regards Muhammad (A.D. 560-632) as the last and greatest of God's prophets and therefore sees Judaism and Christianity as corruptions of the true way. During his lifetime Muhammad united all the tribes of Arabia in the worship of his one God, Allah, and within 100 years of his death, this new religion had spread right across North Africa and into Spain.

Largely, however, the Muslim creed that there is no God but Allah and that Muhammad is his prophet, spread by the waging of religious war. Perhaps it is here that the most immediate contrast is seen with the teaching of Jesus. He rejected the way of coercion in religion. Sadly the institutionalized church has often ignored his teaching historically. Nevertheless, it is clear that Jesus would have nothing to do with spreading his gospel by use of force. However, this is not true of Islam. The idea of *Jihad*, or Holy War, against the infidels is preached as a religious duty incumbent on all good Muslims. Whereas the church can properly disassociate itself from, and condemn, the murder gangs of the IRA or the Protestant para-military groups in Northern Ireland, as clearly going against the way of Christ, it is not possible for Islam to do the same with the Islamic terrorist groups of the Middle East. Their religion does try to justify the use of force.

The controversy over Salman Rushdie, who had supposedly insulted Islam in his book *The Satanic Verses*, resulted in the issue of a sentence of death against the author. Here again is highlighted the use of coercion by Islam. Here, for me, is bad fruit which indicates that Islam is a bad tree.

This is not to say there are not many noble and valuable

aspects to Islam. Organizations like the Red Crescent are engaged in many good works of compassion and mercy. But the idea that force can be used to coerce religious belief is rooted in the very origins of Islam. In fact this seems to spring from Islam's basic concept of God. Whereas the great emphasis of Christianity is on God as the God who so *loved* the world that he gave his only Son to rescue us, the Islamic view of God is rather different. Allah is viewed as very high and very holy. There is great stress on the 'otherness' of Allah. Whereas the holy and high God of the Bible became man and walked among us in the person of Jesus, such an idea would be impossible for Allah. He is distant. He is unapproachable. But when there is so much stress on the otherness of God and the complete difference between God and his creatures, it becomes very difficult to see what God and men have in common.

The Lord Jesus Christ tells us that the greatest need of man is to come to know and experience God: 'This is eternal life: that they may know you, the only true God, and Jesus Christ, whom you have sent' (John 17:3). By contrast it is not really possible to know the God of Islam. In fact the great command of Islam is not first of all to love God, but rather it is framed in terms only of submission to him. The word 'Islam' means submission. Al-Junayd, a ninth-century Muslim mystic, writes saying, 'No one knows God save himself, most high and therefore even to the best of his creatures he has only revealed his names in which he hides himself.'

It is worth contrasting those words with the words of Jesus: 'No one knows the Father except the Son and those to whom the Son chooses to reveal him' (Matthew 11:27). Here Jesus tells us that men and women can come through himself not just to revere God as a far distant almighty deity, but to *know* God, and not just to know him, but to know him as their *Father*. Jesus speaks therefore of a deep and loving relationship with the living God which is rather different from the way that Islam offers. It seems to me that the human spirit needs something more than reverence for an almighty God. We need to know the love of God. Thus it is that having spoken of knowing God, Jesus was able to go on to say, 'Come to me, all you who are weary and burdened, and I will give you rest. Take my yoke upon you and learn from me, for I am gentle and humble in heart, and you will find rest for your souls. For my yoke is easy and my burden is light' (Matthew 11:28-30).

## Judaism

Throughout the world we find Jewish communities, and the history of the Jewish people and their religion is most interesting. Jesus was a Jew. The Jews trace their religion back to their forefathers and therefore Christians and Jews have in common the Old Testament Scriptures and a faith in the Messiah. The difference is that whereas the Christian says that the Messiah has come, in the person of Jesus, followers of Judaism reject this idea and are still waiting for the Messiah.

Now, as I understand it, Jesus has fulfilled the Old Testament prophecies concerning the Messiah in a most dramatic and unmistakable way. But the Jews argue against this. I think they are wrong, but nevertheless let us respect their view and for the moment try to put ourselves in Jewish shoes as those who are still waiting for the Messiah. It is here that for me their argument breaks down.

For example, the Old Testament makes it plain that when he came the Messiah would be a direct descendant of King David, from the tribe of Judah. To David God promised a descendant of whom the Lord said, 'I will set him over my house and my kingdom for ever' (1 Chronicles 17:14). '"The days are coming," declares the Lord, "when I will raise up to David a righteous Branch, a King who will reign wisely and do what is just and right in the land ... "' (Jeremiah 23:5). 'A shoot will come up from the stump of Jesse [David's father]; from his roots a Branch will bear fruit. The Spirit of the Lord will rest on him ...' (Isaiah 11:1-2). So the Jews still wait for a Messiah of the house of David. But as I understand it, it would now be impossible to prove with certainty who, if anyone, belongs to the house of David today, since the genealogical records and family trees of the Jewish nation were destroyed when Jerusalem was sacked by the Romans in A.D. 70. Yet Jesus was of the house and lineage of David (Luke 2:4).

Again, concerning the Messiah, the Old Testament prophet Malachi predicted, 'Suddenly the Lord you are seeking will come to his temple; the messenger of the covenant, whom you desire, will come' (Malachi 3:1). Now Jesus certainly did come to the Jewish temple in Jerusalem that Malachi knew. Jesus was brought there even as a baby and in later years often preached there. But that temple was destroyed in A.D. 70, so it is impossible for any future Messiah to fulfil this prophecy. It is impossible for the temple to be rebuilt in Jerusalem at present for the Muslim mosque known as the Dome of the Rock now stands on the spot where the temple was built in ancient times. No doubt some will argue that we should not be looking for too literal a fulfilment of such prophecies today. But when Jesus has already fulfilled them in a most concrete and obvious way it is hard to ignore his claim to be the true Messiah.

The prophet Micah predicted that the Messiah is to be born in Bethlehem:

'But you, Bethlehem Ephrathah,
    though you are small among the clans of Judah,
out of you will come for me,
    one who will be ruler over Israel,
whose origins are from of old,
    from ancient times'

(Micah 5:2)

Are we really to be waiting for another Christmas in Bethlehem? No. Judaism in many ways has much to commend it, but it is,

## Jesus and other religions

for me, the religion that lost its way. The Messiah has come, but his own people, the Jews, rejected him, and are unwilling to face their mistake.

The Jews are fine people and Jewish thinkers and artists have made great and wonderful contributions to civilization and in many ways have enriched our world. Anti-Semitism is an outrageous and terrible thing and should be rejected and condemned with horror. But to disagree with the Jews is not to be anti-Semitic. We can disagree without malice. It seems to me that the Jews have got it wrong. The Messiah is Jesus, who even now through his gospel is what the Old Testament predicted he would be: the Servant of the Lord who is the 'light for the Gentiles' (Isaiah 49:6), bringing God's salvation to the ends of the earth.

### Bible cults

Over the last few centuries a number of cults have grown up within the Christian church and then split away from it, forming their own religion. The most well known of these are groups like the Mormons, the Christadelphians and the Jehovah's Witnesses. It is interesting that they all have one thing in common. Each of them is unitarian. In other words, they deny the Christian doctrine of the Trinity, of one God in three persons, Father, Son and Holy Spirit. In particular, they deny the deity of the Lord Jesus Christ as the Son of God.

Yet if we look through the New Testament it is quite obvious that Jesus was regarded as God by the first disciples. On meeting with the risen Lord Jesus, Thomas, the disciple who doubted, had all his doubts swept away and found himself acknowledging Jesus as 'my Lord and my God!' (John 20:28). It was even clear to those who were not followers of Jesus that he claimed to be God become man. On one occasion Jesus challenged the unbelieving Jews as to why they were persecuting him: '"I have shown you many great miracles from the

Father. For which of these do you stone me?" "We are not stoning you for any of these," replied the Jews, "but for blasphemy, because you, a mere man, claim to be God"' (John 10:32-33). Such verses as these contradict what the cults say of Jesus. In an attempt to get around such things the Jehovah's Witnesses actually use their own special version of the Bible, called the New World Translation, which changes the accepted meanings of the Bible text. If they base their beliefs on the Bible, then they should be true to the Bible. Here is a lack of fundamental integrity.

*The New Age Movement*

In many ways the rise of the so-called New Age Movement is most interesting. It indicates the presence of a great spiritual hunger in the hearts of modern men and women. At the end of the twentieth century, which has seen science and technology and general wealth among people come to a zenith, it would seem that mere materialism cannot satisfy the inner life of man and this movement, which is rather a hotch-potch of Eastern ideas, magic and myths, has sprung up right in the centre of modern Western culture.

Under the New Age Movement canopy a vast range of ideas are embraced: meditation, yoga, Buddhism, mysticism, Hinduism, evolution, vegetarianism, human rights and animal welfare, paranormal phenomena, astrology and reincarnation, to name but a few. Pertinent to the theme of this book, it is interesting to find that within the New Age there is a very strong emphasis on 'the unity of all things' and what is called 'the one life'. As pointed out in the first chapter, the spirit of our age is for one world, and here is a spiritual movement which has captured that spirit.

Much more could be written, and has been written, from a Christian point of view about the New Age Movement. Many of the practices involved are roundly condemned by the Bible

## Jesus and other religions

as occult and sinful, and it cannot be stressed too much how spiritually dangerous this movement is to people.

But talking on its own terms for a moment, what can be said briefly? Strongly rooted in the pantheistic idea that everything is God, the focus of the New Age Movement seems to be to lead people into an awareness of themselves as divine beings. It is very attractive in the sense of being very affirming for the individual. With all seriousness New Age devotees teach that human beings are God. What could be more of a boost to one's personal ego? Also, of course, the realization that you are God at once neutralizes any anxiety — provoking ideas such as personal accountability for one's actions! Furthermore believing oneself to be God implies that one is inherently good. The most well-known proponent of the New Age Movement has been the actress Shirley MacLaine. In her book *Dancing in the light* she writes, 'I know that I exist, therefore I am. I know that the godsource exists, therefore it is. Since I am part of that force, I am that I am.' The phrase 'I am that I am', is actually the name by which God revealed himself to Moses when he called him to lead his people out of slavery in Egypt. To accept the ideas of the New Age is to replace God by ourselves. Taking New Age on its own terms, the simple question which occurs is this: how can this possibly work out in real life? For example, how can two people who both believe they are God possibly live together? When there is an argument, as real life dictates there will be, who backs down? Which one can possibly admit to being wrong if they are both supposed to be inherently good? Because a person believes that he or she is God, does that mean that this person believes that he or she must dominate in all relationships with other people, or indeed ignore the laws of a country and its judiciary? And how does this 'God' account for things like a headache, or worse still, cope with cancer? Can 'God' do nothing about death? Or is it that the god of the New Age is not God at all?

Again, it seems to me that the New Age Movement is a

world of very attractive but very dangerous make-believe. Unreality is untruth, and untruth is just another name for the bad fruit of lies.

## Christianity and the world

It would be stupid to say that Christianity has never made any mistakes. For a start, not everything that goes under the label of 'Christianity' is what it claims to be. Jesus himself warned of wolves in sheep's clothing and deceivers who use his name to gain their own ends. Also true Christians have made many blunders down the centuries of church history. In a way that is to be expected, for the true church has never claimed to be anything other than a collection of sinners — sinners who have been rescued not because they are better than anyone else, but because of the pure grace and kindness of God. However, having voiced that caveat, it seems to me that there is a case to be made for much 'good fruit' which Christians have produced in the world. And by Christians I mean not just groups who use the name of Christ, or even groups who wave a Bible under people's noses, but people who do sincerely seek to practise the teachings of Jesus.

First of all, no political or religious movement has been totally beneficial to the world. But if any movement has a proper claim to have been the most beneficial movement for mankind, Christianity has a right to that claim. To follow the history of Bible-believing, Christian faith is a most interesting story. Along its path you will find the beginnings of such things as hospitals and general education for people. It was, as we have said, out of a Christian context that modern science developed, with all the benefits it has brought to the world. It was not from Buddhism or atheism, but from Christianity that our technological society sprang. The roots of political democracy and freedom for the individual under the law, which we

## Jesus and other religions

all value so highly, grew up out of Christian soil. It was the Eastern worlds of Islam and Hinduism which persisted with the rule of earthly potentates. Again, slavery was a scourge of the world in both East and West, but it was through the continuing struggles of Christian people like William Wilberforce that slavery was finally abolished.

Secondly, and perhaps more importantly, it is not just in the big realms of science and health and freedom that Christianity has been the seedbed of progress, but in perhaps the more important realm of the lives of individuals that it has been so beneficial down the years. Many of the great religions are religions into which people are born by dint of being born in a certain area of the world. But true Christianity comes not by natural birth, but by spiritual birth. Christianity is a religion of conversion, and that conversion changes people's lives, it would seem as nothing else on earth can do. Countless people have been rescued from lives of degradation and personal hopelessness by the power of the gospel of Jesus Christ. The following true story illustrates this point well.

Early in his ministry the evangelist and Bible teacher Dr Harry Ironside was living in the San Francisco Bay area working with a group of believers called 'Brethren'. One Sunday as he was walking through the city he came upon a group of Salvation Army workers holding a meeting on the corner of Market and Grant Avenues. There were probably sixty of them. When they recognized Ironside they immediately asked him if he would give his testimony. So he did, giving a word about how God had saved him through faith in the bodily death and literal resurrection of Jesus.

As he was speaking, Ironside noticed that on the edge of the crowd a well-dressed man had taken a card from his pocket and written something on it. As Ironside finished his talk this man came forward, lifted his hat and very politely handed him the card. On one side was his name, which Ironside immediately recognized. The man was one of the early socialists who had made a name for himself lecturing not only for socialism but also against Christianity. As Ironside turned the card over, he read, 'Sir, I challenge you to debate with me the question "Agnosticism versus Christianity" in the Academy of Science Hall next Sunday afternoon at four o'clock. I will pay all expenses.'

Ironside reread the card aloud and then replied somewhat like this: 'I am very much interested in this challenge... Therefore I will be glad to agree to this debate on the following conditions: namely, that in order to prove that Mr ——— has something worth fighting for and worth debating about, he will promise to bring with him to the Hall next Sunday two people, whose qualifications I will give in a moment, as proof that agnosticism is of real value in changing human lives and building true character.

'First he must promise to bring with him one man who was for years what we commonly call a "down-and-outer". I am not particular as to the exact nature of the sins that had wrecked his life and made him an outcast from society — whether a drunkard, or a criminal of some kind, or a victim of his sensual appetite — but a man who for years was under the power of evil habits from which he could not deliver himself, but who on some occasion entered one of Mr ———'s meetings and heard his glorification of agnosticism and his denunciations of the Bible and Christianity, and whose heart and mind as he listened to such an address were so deeply stirred that he went away from that meeting saying, "Henceforth I too am an agnostic," and as a result of imbibing that particular philosophy found that a new power had come into his life. The sins he once loved he now hates and righteousness and goodness are now the ideals of his life. He is now an entirely new man, a credit to himself and an asset to society — all because he is an agnostic.

'Secondly, I would like Mr ——— to promise to bring with him one woman — and I think he may have more difficulty in finding the woman than the man — who was once a poor,

## Jesus and other religions

wrecked, characterless outcast, the slave of evil passions, and the victim of man's corrupt living, perhaps one who had lived for years in some evil resort ... utterly lost, ruined and wretched because of her life of sin. But this woman also entered a hall where Mr ——— was loudly proclaiming his agnosticism and ridiculing the message of the Holy Scriptures. As she listened, hope was born in her heart, and she said, "This is just what I need to deliver me from the slavery of sin!" She followed the teaching and became an intelligent agnostic or infidel. As a result, her whole being revolted against the degradation of the life she had been living. She fled from the den of iniquity where she had been held captive so long and today, rehabilitated, she has won her way back to an honoured position in society and is living a clean, virtuous, happy life — all because she is an agnostic.

'Now,' he said, addressing the gentleman who had presented him with his card and the challenge, 'if you will promise to bring these two people with you as examples of what agnosticism can do, I will promise to meet you at the Hall of Science at four o'clock next Sunday and I will bring with me at the very least 100 men and women who for years lived in just such sinful degradation as I have tried to depict, but who have been gloriously saved through believing the gospel which you ridicule. I will have these men and women with me on the platform as witnesses to the miraculous saving power of Jesus Christ and as present-day proof of the truth of the Bible.'

Dr Ironside then turned to the Salvation Army captain, a woman, and said, 'Captain, have you any who could go with me to such a meeting?'

She exclaimed with enthusiasm, 'We can give you forty at least just from this one corps, and we will give you a brass band to lead the procession!'

'Fine,' Dr Ironside answered. 'Now, Mr ———, I will have no difficulty in picking up sixty others from the various missions, gospel halls, and evangelical churches of the city;

and if you will promise faithfully to bring two such exhibits as I have described, I will come marching in at the head of such a procession, with the band playing "Onward Christian Soldiers" and I will be ready for the debate.'

Apparently the man who had made the challenge must have had some sense of humour, for he smiled wryly and waved his hand in a depreciating kind of way as if to say, 'Nothing doing!' and then edged out of the crowd while the bystanders clapped for Ironside and the others.[3]

But not only has Christianity the good fruit of its beneficial effects both on the broad canvas of social well-being and the smaller canvas of individual lives; there is another factor which is well worth considering as we look at evidence of its uniqueness and truthfulness. A third major reason which points to Christianity as the way for the world is that it has a substantial claim to be the only truly universal religion. It is the only faith which has found, and is finding, acceptance on a worldwide scale. The other religions are very much either restricted to certain geographical areas or associated with particular ethnic groups. Hinduism and Buddhism are mainly found still in Asia. The Islamic faith is still by and large confined to Arabs and folk from Malaysia and the Indian subcontinent. Indeed this is remarkable, for Islam has spent much energy and finance in seeking to export itself into the West. Yet although many mosques have appeared in our cities, the adherents of Islam in the West have generally arrived by immigration and birth, not by conversion. By contrast, Christianity has taken root and prospered in every single culture and area of the world. The last 100 years have seen vast numbers of people in Africa, South East Asia and South America being converted to Christ. In fact, this has occurred on such a scale that it could be said that the centre of gravity of the Christian world is no longer, as was historically the case, in the northern hemisphere, but has swung down to the developing countries of the southern hemisphere. These geographical facts about

# Jesus and other religions

the spread of Christianity not only cause Christianity to stand out among the world faiths, but are also particularly interesting in the light of the constant predictions throughout the Bible that the salvation it proclaims will spread to all the nations of the earth. Jesus Christ is proclaimed as the universal Saviour, the Lamb of God who takes away the sin of the world (John 1:29).

## Back to the elephant

We began our chapter with the well-known story of the blind men, the elephant and the king. On the surface it seems a helpful analogy concerning the relationships between the religions of the world, but on further investigation we have found that this analogy will not hold water in the face of the facts.

Not only is this so, but as I said earlier, actually the story itself, although extremely plausible, contains a grave fallacy and any person who uses it to argue for pluralism and the unity of all religions is, perhaps unwittingly, being extremely arrogant. What do I mean?

The fallacy lies in that the story is told from the point of view of the king, who is not blind but can see what the blind men cannot. He can see the elephant and can see that the blind men are unable to grasp the full reality of the elephant and are only able to get hold of part of the truth. The story is constantly told in order to neutralize the affirmation of certainty concerning God, and to suggest that people learn to recognize that none of them has more than one aspect of truth. But, actually, the real point of the story is exactly the opposite. If the king were also blind there would be no story. The story is told by the king and it is the immensely arrogant claim of the pluralist to be the one who sees the full truth which all the world's religions are only groping after. Actually, of course, the advocate of pluralism is just as blind as any other human being.

But another point to be made is that we may say that the position of the king in this story is claimed by Jesus. What we cannot see, he says he is able to see. What ordinary people like ourselves dare not claim, he does claim. He claims, as the Son of God, sent from heaven, to see clearly what all others are blind to.

Jesus has produced his credentials to substantiate this claim, not least in his miracles, resurrection and the spread of his church worldwide according to his predictions. But who else dare claim that they can see what others cannot?

# 6.
# The road to freedom

There is a virtuous motive behind the pluralist vision of one world. All people of good will surely desire to see all their fellow men at one, with enough food and clothing, education and housing to have the liberty to fulfil their potential as human beings and enjoy their lives. Such sentiments stand enshrined, for example, in these most famous lines from the Declaration of Independence of the United States of 1776: 'We hold these truths to be self-evident, that all men are created equal, that they are endowed by their Creator with certain unalienable rights, that among these are life, liberty and the pursuit of happiness. That to secure these rights, governments are instituted among men, deriving their just powers from the consent of the governed ...'

The biblical language finds an echo in all our hearts as it speaks of a perfect world in terms of a restful, pastoral scene of peace:

> 'They will beat their swords into ploughshares
>     and their spears into pruning hooks.
> Nation will not take up sword against nation,
>     nor will they train for war any more.
> Every man will sit under his own vine
>     and under his own fig-tree,
> and no one will make them afraid'
>
> (Micah 4:3-4).

This vision of peace and fulfilment for all humanity is inextricably tied up with the idea of personal freedom. This concept is of vast importance. How can people be happy unless they have liberty? How can an individual enjoy life unless he or she is free to think and to take whatever opportunities come? It is the rightness of such fundamental principles which has driven on brave men and women of history to stand against slavery and other forms of oppression. It is the absolute propriety of human dignity and individual freedom which has lent courage to those who have fought for civil rights, and has brought about the overthrow of apartheid and Communism in our century. The cry for freedom is the cry of the human soul. But a superficial view of personal freedom is leading our modern world into great trouble. We need to think carefully about what we mean by freedom.

There are two kinds of freedom we can identify. These two types of freedom may be epitomized in the ideas of graffiti and of gymnastics. 'Graffiti freedom,' as I may term it, is a freedom which is formless. The man with the spray-can in the subway just sprays upon the wall whatever is uppermost in his mind at that particular moment. It is a freedom that strikes out against rules and the status quo. It is a freedom that is self-centred. It is a freedom that is essentially lawless and anarchic, a freedom that costs nothing and is often destructive. The freedom of the gymnast is very different. The gymnast is a person who is free to perform the most wonderful acrobatic feats and thrill the crowd with marvellous strength and agility. He or she is free to do things which others cannot. However, the gymnast has achieved that freedom, not by an anarchic approach to life, but by training. It has cost him or her a great deal to achieve this ability. The gymnast is free to move and leap in a way which others cannot because of hard work and following the rules. Behind that dynamic performance are years of discipline concerning diet and muscle exercise. Behind that freedom of expression on the gymnasium floor are hours of toil and sweat

## The road to freedom

and learning from coaches and master athletes. There are, then, these two kinds of freedom, and the difference between them is crucial. One is lawless; the other is freedom based on law.

The problem for the modern world, especially in the West, is that when we speak about personal freedom it is the graffiti freedom ideal which often underlies our assumptions. The gymnast is free to explore the vast array of possibilities within the limitations of the capabilities of the human frame. But it is not this kind of freedom to which the twentieth century aspires. The spirit of our times desires an individual freedom without form, a freedom without limits.

It is this point of view which lies behind, for example, much of the direction of the modern cinema. The whole genre of modern films embraces situations where 'anything can happen', whether it is in terms of violence, fantasy, or whatever. We are fascinated by 'no limits' situations. The same view of freedom underpins the explosion of the drug culture in the modern world. Drugs enable people to feel good, even when circumstances are bad. They take people beyond the limits for a time. And people are sadly willing to expose themselves to the detrimental physical effects of the drugs just for the thrill, for the moment of 'freedom'. Again it is this view of freedom which has inspired the sexual revolution of the last twenty years. 'Why should I be limited to one partner?' people ask. 'Why should I be limited to a partner of the opposite sex?' Freedom means no limits. With such an outlook it is not surprising also that money becomes the god of the age, for money brings freedom. Money gives the power of autonomy to its owner. The rich man can go where he likes and to a large extent do what he likes.

Whereas the art of the gymnast is to explore the possibilities of creativity within boundaries, graffiti style freedom questions all limits. Indeed for our age it has become almost a moral imperative that limits are intrinsically evil. For example, these quotations from the novelist D. H. Lawrence, who is one of the great architects of the twentieth-century mindset, carry this connotation:

> Evil, what is evil?
> There is only one evil, to deny life,
> as Rome denied Etruvia and
> mechanical America Montsezuma still.[1]

> Morality which is based on ideas,
> or on an ideal, is an unmitigated evil.[2]

This, of course, all springs from the atheistic, this-worldly assumption of our times adopted by people like Lawrence. If this life is all, and when it is over that is the end, then surely a human being must be given every opportunity to do whatever pleases and thrills him or her. You only have one life. Anything which holds back the individual is seen as unfair. A person must be given as much autonomy as possible. It is at this point that the whole pluralistic approach comes in. It is here that the argument is made that to insist on absolute religious truth is restrictive and therefore improper. People need to be able to make their own rules for living, to choose their own 'truth'. Only then are they truly free!

But this view leads directly into great trouble, as Western society is beginning to find out. It leads to trouble both for the individual and for society in general.

For the individual this view of freedom is disastrous firstly because its goal is ultimately impossible. If real freedom means breaking all limits, a person must reach for the sky. A limited man must achieve the limitless to find fulfilment. The finite creature must encompass the infinite. This is an impossibility. Therefore fulfilment must forever elude us. This view of freedom leaves individuals forever disappointed. It is a recipe for the personal emptiness, disillusionment, and desperation which pervade our modern culture. Secondly, it is disastrous,

# The road to freedom

simply because the world is not like that. The world we live in is a world with limits governed by all kinds of laws, scientific laws not least, and we break these laws at our peril. This view of freedom ever strives to go beyond the limit. We may be free to choose to try to go beyond the limits of law, but disastrously we are not free to choose the consequences of our choice. The world is just not like that. We may choose to experience what it is like to jump from a skyscraper, but we are not free to choose the consequences of our action. Similarly, we are free to choose to abandon the norms of family life, but we are not free to choose the emotional consequences of that for our abandoned children. The harvest we reap depends on what we sow. We live in a world governed by laws. That is reality. This view of freedom inevitably leads to hurt and disaster. Fortunately people are not always rational and consistent and so they often fail to take this view of freedom to its logical conclusion. But this ideal is a driving force in our world. It inevitably leads to disaster, for it is a view of freedom which challenges reality itself, and in such a match there can only be one winner.

For society this view of freedom is disastrous too. This is because in a society which idolizes this anarchic view of freedom, inevitably the criminal becomes the hero. It is law that is seen as restrictive. Thus we have seen in the last few years, and will continue to see, the criminal community cast as the heroes of films and novels. It is morals which are portrayed as limiting. Therefore it is the one who is perceived as having the 'courage' to break the law who is applauded as the man who is truly free. He is seen as having the courage to be 'true to himself'. Of course, the true hero is the one who does all this and who doesn't get caught! In the same way this anarchic freedom perverts our perception of family life and the need to care for others. The demands of family life, under the jaundiced eye of 'graffiti freedom', are seen as restrictive. Similarly, the obligations to care for the needy, or for sick relatives, are an additional drain upon our time. Again, I am glad to say, emotional ties often win out in practice over such conclusions, but nevertheless this is the logic of this view of freedom. As we look at the Western world at the end of the twentieth century, it has become a commonplace for commentators to tell us that society is in a bad way. All around we see social disintegration. Our view of freedom, espoused in the early years of this century, has to a large extent brought this about. Our art forms of TV and cinema are full of acclaim for the anti-hero. Our big cities are places of loneliness and anonymity where community has broken down. The Western world, for all its technological advances, is also a place where crime figures seem forever to increase. This is just the logical result of such a view of freedom.

Pluralism has much in common with this view of freedom. Pluralism is basically an approach to belief which wishes to embrace any and every set of ideas of how life is to be lived without discrimination. In this area of belief therefore it inherently denies the idea of truth, of right beliefs and wrong beliefs and of absolute laws for living, for this would set a limit to what is acceptable. Beneath the ideas of pluralism there lies this same disastrous view of freedom. It may be thought that since pluralism stands for this view of freedom only in the area of beliefs its stance is not all that serious. But rather the reverse is true because beliefs govern our attitudes and deeply influence our actions. Our beliefs determine our moral code. As a man believes, so he is. As a man thinks, so he behaves. Pluralism unthinkingly adopts this view of freedom which is proving more and more problematical for the Western world and for its people.

When Jesus speaks about freedom, it should therefore come as no surprise to us that his ideas are very different. His view of freedom, and therefore of fulfilment for the individual, has much more to do with the gymnastic model of freedom. His view of freedom is firmly based not in lawlessness, but in the

# The road to freedom

foundation of truth. One of Christ's most famous sayings about freedom was spoken to a mixed crowd, some of whom were disciples, but not all, and some of whom were on the brink of decision as to whether to follow Jesus or not. To them Jesus said, 'If you hold to my teaching, you are really my disciples. Then you will know the truth, and the truth will set you free' (John 8:31-32).

Fulfilment and freedom do not come by abandoning the possibility of certainty of belief. Rather fulfilment and freedom come by knowing, and living by, the truth. It is commitment to the truth, the truth which has been shown as the truth through the life, death and resurrection of Jesus, that leads to freedom for human beings. God has cut through all the confusion of the conflicting ideas of the darkened human consciousness of mankind by revealing himself through his incomparable Son Jesus, and the gloriously unique historical events surrounding him. It is in Jesus that we find the truth and through commitment to that truth that we find freedom. Just as the gymnast finds freedom by pursuing the laws and disciplines of his sport, so human beings find true freedom, life as it was truly meant to be lived, by committing themselves to Jesus Christ and pursuing his teaching.

Jesus himself is the truth, the living truth (John 14:6), and God's Word the Bible, is the written truth (John 17:17). What is it to be a true Christian? What is it to be a truly free human being? It is a matter of an utter, thorough and continuing commitment to the truth of Jesus.

We will look at this matter of being committed to the truth.

## Reasons for commitment to truth

Here are three reasons which reiterate why we need as human beings to be committed to Jesus, who is the truth.

1. *Because we were made for truth*

God is there and God is our Maker. The reason why our world is a world of laws and limits is because that is the way God has made the world. It is not a world of chance and ultimate chaos. The laws of the world, the physical laws and the moral laws, are part of the Maker's instructions. We are made by God and were made to function according to our Maker's instructions. We function best when we obey him. The Maker's instructions are not optional; there is no other way. To ignore them is to bring disaster.

I learnt this soon after I got married. We had been given a cream-making attachment for our food mixer. We used it and I washed it up and fitted it back together as I thought it should go, taking no notice of the instruction leaflet. The next time we used it, there was a screeching of metal and the appliance snapped and was broken! Similarly, we ignore the truth, our Maker's instructions, at our peril.

We were made for truth. The God who made us is the God who came in the person of Jesus. The God who formed man out of the dust of the earth and breathed into him the breath of life is that same God who spoke and breathed out his Word, the Bible. So we match. People and truth are made for each other, for the same God is behind them both.

Or to put it another way, God originally made us in his image. We were made as finite reflections of the infinite God. Now God's character is plainly revealed in Jesus. God's character is also clearly set forth in the Scriptures. When God's character and people are brought together we are being re-shaped into the mould we were originally made from. The pressures and sins of a fallen world have distorted us and ruined us as personalities. But when God's character is impressed again upon our personalities we find ourselves being reformed into what we were made to be. We find a deep sense of at last being at home with ourselves. Why commit ourselves

# The road to freedom

to the truth? Because we were made for truth. Only here can we find our feet upon solid ground. Only here with Jesus do we find the truth which touches our spirits and breathes true peace.

## 2. *Because the truth of God is sent to us in love*

Jesus' teaching is the teaching of one who truly loves us. The nineteenth-century American preacher Charles Finney had a good definition of love. He said love means bringing about the highest possible good in another person's life. That is a proper description of God's love for us. Christ loves people. Even in our sins he still loves us.

At the beginning of the chapter in John's Gospel where Jesus talks about freedom there is an incident recorded in which a woman who was surprised in the very act of adultery was brought before Jesus. It is worth reading: 'But Jesus went to the Mount of Olives. At dawn he appeared again in the temple courts, where all the people gathered round him, and he sat down to teach them. The teachers of the law and the Pharisees brought in a woman caught in adultery. They made her stand before the group and said to Jesus, "Teacher, this woman was caught in the act of adultery. In the Law Moses commanded us to stone such women. Now what do you say?" They were using this question as a trap, in order to have a basis for accusing him. But Jesus bent down and started to write on the ground with his finger. When they kept on questioning him, he straightened up and said to them, "If any one of you is without sin, let him be the first to throw a stone at her." Again he stooped down and wrote on the ground. At this, those who heard began to go away one at a time, the older ones first, until only Jesus was left, with the woman still standing there. Jesus straightened up and asked her, "Woman, where are they? Has no one condemned you?" "No one sir," she said. "Then neither do I condemn you," Jesus declared. "Go now and leave your life of sin"' (John 8:1-11).

How this incident speaks of the love of Jesus! The Pharisees just wanted to use the woman, to embarrass her, to condemn her. They wanted to use her to see if they could trip Jesus. Was Jesus on the side of morality or not? Jesus pulls no punches with the woman. He says to her in effect, 'You have got to face it, this life of yours is wretched and no good.' But at the same time he turns the situation so that her accusers are silenced and she is saved. He exposes sin, but his love shines through. When the Pharisees have gone he says, 'Neither do I condemn you. Go and sin no more.' It is a word of love which no doubt renewed that woman's life. He wanted the best for her. The truth comes to us, deeply with a love which is given its full expression in the self-sacrifice of the cross. This is why we should commit ourselves to the truth.

As an expansion on this point, it is worth referring back to the example we used of the machine and the maker's instructions, in order to understand something more about God's commands and his love. Of course, people are not machines. There are great differences between a set of instructions for an electrical appliance and God's instructions for mankind. A machine is not a conscious being; a person is. A machine has no will of its own, no freedom for creative thought. So it is that the rules governing a machine's use are very restricted and almost rigid in their nature. The appliance can only be used according to a very narrow path of possibilities, with often a fixed sequence of instructions. Because we are not machines God's instructions for mankind are not like that. Rather God's laws are laws which give us freedom within broad limits. This was reflected in his first command to Adam and Eve. They were free to eat any fruit in the garden except just one. They could choose a wide variety of possibilities. There was freedom within a limit. Again the Ten Commandments, for example, set limits to human behaviour — no lying, no adultery, etc. — but within these negatives there is a vast free area of positive life and activity which

# The road to freedom

human beings are at liberty to enjoy and explore creatively. God our Maker wants us to use our image-of-God creativity within the boundaries which he has set down for our good. He loves us. This is why as our Maker he informs us of the limits. To go beyond those limits will bring hurt and disaster. But within those boundaries is where we were designed to function and enjoy our lives. Again God's great command is for us sinners to believe on the Lord Jesus Christ and so be saved. We are to become disciples of Jesus. But the Christian life is not life in a strait-jacket. Although every Christian's life has certain fundamental elements, which are the same for any Christian, not every Christian life is exactly the same. Christians are not clones. Within the boundaries of Christian discipleship there is infinite possibility and variety of life. God's truth is given to us because God loves us. Therefore, it is safe to commit our lives to the truth.

3. *Because God's truth has the solution for every problem we experience*

Please do not get me wrong. I do not mean that on our committing ourselves to follow Christ life becomes a bed of roses. Far from it; we live in a fallen world, where sin and trials will continue to confront us. But I do mean that, with the aid of God's truth, whatever our circumstances, whatever tough times we face, we can find contentment, peace and hope.

How can it be that this one book, the Bible, the teaching of Jesus, can speak to every possible human situation? It is God's Word and God's Word is full of power. In the beginning God spoke and out of nothing all the world came into existence. That is a picture to us of the unlimited potency of the Word of God.

The Bible is a true record of God's dealings with mankind. But it is not just a true record. Within the true record is truth for life. For example, there is in the Old Testament the true record of David's sin with Bathsheba. That adultery really happened.

But within that story is the truth that sincere repentance leads to forgiveness and life. Or again, in the New Testament there is the true record of our Lord Jesus Christ performing the miracle of stilling the storm on the Sea of Galilee. That miracle actually took place. But that story also points us to the truth that Jesus is Lord over all creation, and situations which are beyond men to cope with can be handled by the Lord Jesus Christ. The story directs us to faith in him for our daily lives. We will find ourselves secure and safe in his hands. Such is the unlimited potency of the truth of God that even when some problems are not directly addressed by Scripture (e.g. experiencing redundancy), yet there are principles and promises in God's Word which the Holy Spirit can uncover for us and illuminate for us, which speak to every situation. The Bible is factually true, but it is also living truth which speaks right into the here and now. The apostle Paul was unjustly in prison and yet he was honestly able to find peace there. He could say, 'I have learned the secret of being content in any and every situation, whether well fed or hungry, whether living in plenty or in want. I can do everything through him who gives me strength' (Philippians 4:12-13).

In Christ, God has supplied us, says the apostle Peter, with 'everything we need for life and godliness' (2 Peter 1:3). Through the Scripture truth, says the apostle Paul, 'the man of God may be thoroughly equipped for every good work' (2 Timothy 3:17). So here is another reason for committing ourselves to Jesus, and following the truth. Because whatever our circumstances, God's truth has an answer which can give us strength to live and enable us to find peace.

Here, then, are some reasons for heeding Jesus' words to hold to his teaching and truly be his disciples. Christ's teaching is the truth of God, its principles are not optional, it is sent to us in love and its application to our lives will bring us into a place of calm contentment.

## Requirements of commitment to truth

We have spoken of committing ourselves to the truth, to following Jesus and his teaching. But what does this involve? What is required of us?

Jesus said, 'If you hold to my teaching you really are my disciples' (John 8:31). That translation is good. People need to hold to Jesus' teaching. They need to learn it and put it into practice, trusting the living Lord Jesus for the consequences. They need to hold on to that teaching, persevere and continue with it, even in the face of opposition and trouble. That is absolutely right. But there is more to it. The original language in which the New Testament was written carries an additional meaning. The original words can be translated, 'If you *abide in* my teaching'. What is the difference? It is right and good for us to hold the truth, but it is another thing for the truth to hold us. It is one thing for truth to abide in our hearts and minds, but it is another thing for our hearts and minds to abide in the truth.

Let me put it like this. It is one thing to hold views and opinions. People usually do. And often they use those views and opinions as vehicles for their own egos. A man may love to tell you his views on politics, or golf, or whatever. What he is often doing is showing you his cleverness. Sadly, it is even possible to do the same thing with the teaching of Jesus. Folk can talk of the Scriptures and of God. But what they are really doing is saying to us, 'Look how much theology I know; look how much of the Bible I can call to memory.' In a sense they 'hold the truth'. But that, of course, is not what Jesus is talking about. They hold it wrongly. We must know the truth, but the truth is not to be a vehicle for us, rather the other way around. It should be that we have so happily received the truth and submitted to it in delight that the truth has taken us up. We are vehicles for it. We are so thrilled with what we have found in Jesus that having thoughtfully received it, we wish humbly not to direct others to ourselves, but to the truth. That is how it should be. Truth has become our home. We do not just hold it, but it holds us. That gives us more of the flavour of what Jesus is speaking of when he exhorts us to hold to his teaching.

How does this happen in a person's life? How does truth come to so grip us? In understanding this we need to see that biblically there are three aspects to truth. Truth is propositional, personal and practical.

## 1. *Truth is propositional*

Christ's teaching is to be received intelligently and thought through carefully. It is to be received first of all as objectively true. God does not brainwash people. He requires the honest use of the critical faculties with which he has endowed us in receiving his Word. But as we investigate God's Word we shall find that we have far more reason to believe that God is reliable in what he says than to believe any fallible, fallen man. So when, for example, it speaks of Jesus being born of a virgin, it is telling us that it really happened like that. We may not understand how, but we understand that God is the God of miracles. Again when the Bible tells us that 'Everyone who calls on the name of the Lord will be saved,' that is the truth. It is a statement of fact which we accept with our minds.

It is absolutely necessary to hold to Christ's teaching as propositional truth. But having said that, we must realize that it cannot be left just at that level. Truth must be received with the mind, but it must go beyond that.

## 2. *Truth is personal*

What we receive as fact we must allow to move us personally. Truth must not just be acknowledged but received into our lives. What God has said, I will take as true for me. The Lord has commanded us to believe on the Lord Jesus Christ (1 John 3:23). Then we say, 'I will believe. I will trust Christ as my

# The road to freedom

Master and Friend.' Scripture tells us that Christ loves sinners. Then we say, 'I will accept that he loves me.' Scripture enjoins us to deny ourselves, take up the cross and follow Christ. We honestly resolve to deny ourselves and, whatever the cost, to follow Jesus. God's truth needs to find a place not just in our heads, but in our hearts. We need to allow the truth to take hold of us and capture our hearts. We need to pray that God's Holy Spirit would so work in us that we do not just know the truth, but honestly love God and love the truth. Jesus calls us to delight ourselves in God and to seek in him the fulfilment of our deepest desires. 'If any one is thirsty,' said Jesus, 'let him come to me and drink.' There can be no true holding of the truth without this personal reception of the truth and personal affection for the truth. Have you received the truth of Christ in this way? Will you do so? As the truth is received in this way it will inevitably lead us further.

## 3. *Truth is practical*

Christ's teaching must be worked out in our lives. We must not simply believe it and love it inwardly, but sincerely put it into practice in our behaviour. Christ's great commands are to love and holiness: 'A new command I give you: Love one another. As I have loved you, so you must love one another' (John 13:34). Christ's love took him all the way to the cross for us and if we are really his disciples then a sacrificial love for others will begin to characterize our lives. Again Jesus said, 'Blessed are those who hunger and thirst for righteousness for they will be filled' (Matthew 5:6). He commands his people to be pure and honest in their lives and to be just and honourable in all their relationships. Of course, the Christian will never be perfect. We shall often fail and there is forgiveness in Christ for our failures. But we sincerely do seek to live lives of love and purity in practical consecration to Christ. The teaching of Jesus must be worked out through our hands and feet and lips if we are truly his disciples.

This is what it is to hold the truth, to abide in the teaching of Jesus. It is not just to hold a few ideas, but to allow our whole life to be shaped by Christ, our Master and Friend. Do you have this thorough commitment to Jesus Christ?

Someone might say, 'Follow Christ's teaching, yes, but there is so much to learn. How can I suddenly put it all into practice?' Obviously the Christian life is a life of learning. We have to take a little at a time and receive and seek to practise the portions we learn as we go along. We cannot do it all at once. But at the beginning of the Christian life a decisive step is taken. It is the step of trusting Christ and surrendering our lives to his mastery. We do not know everything, but we sincerely put ourselves at his disposal, and putting the past behind us, are now ready to be lifelong learners from Jesus. We trust him first of all for the forgiveness of our sins and our personal salvation. But such trust inevitably leads us to learn from him and follow him in our everyday lives. We take the commands of the New Testament and seek to live according to them. Does Jesus teach that 'It is more blessed to give than to receive'? Then we will follow his command and let that affect the way we conduct our finances and trust him for the consequences. Does the Scripture tell us that we should turn our anxieties into prayer, being careful to thank God for the good things we do have? Then we take that to ourselves. We seek to practise that and hold onto it in the face of life.

All this can be summarized in a helpful little equation which I learned.[3] The formula may help those who are of a mathematical bent to grasp what it is to be a Christian. The equation is:

$R^2 + A^2 =$ a true disciple.

R - recognize the truth
R - relate to the truth personally
A - assimilate the truth into your life
A - act upon the truth in practice

# The road to freedom

Think that through. It gives a good summary of what it is to be a Christian.

Looking at that formula, you need to ask yourself, 'Am I a Christian?' If you are not and realize that you ought to become a Christian, it would be worthwhile reading this section through again. You need to submit your life personally and prayerfully and irreversibly to following Jesus.

In the atmosphere of our pluralistic society, commitment is rare and even where it is present it is often shallow. All kinds of different ideologies and religions are set before us simply as different possible alternative opinions. The impression is given that no one can really be sure that any of them is right. Obviously such an ethos militates against any firm commitment. We are encouraged to take each one with a pinch of salt. We are told to hold things loosely if we are going to hold them at all. But Christ calls us to commitment. The Christian is someone who has become convinced that the way of Christ is not just a possible opinion, but it is actually the truth. He or she is convinced that Jesus is not just a man, but that he is God, and that he loves us and died to save us. In response to these convictions the Christian is one who seriously and thoroughly dedicates himself or herself to following Jesus. This is not easy. In our modern world the Christian will easily be misunderstood and vilified by others. But humbly and lovingly the true disciple will go on and not turn back.

David Livingstone's motto concerning his Christian faith gives us a fine summary of commitment to Christ: 'No reservations. No regrets. No retreat.'

## The results of commitment to the truth

Jesus said, 'If you hold to my teaching you are really my disciples. Then you will know the truth, and the truth will set you free' (John 8:31-32). Here Jesus highlights two promised results of following him.

## 1. *Assurance*

Jesus says to would-be followers, 'You will *know* the truth.' There is a promise of confidence and assurance for life. There is all the difference in the world between having a tentative idea and being certain.

Not long ago I had to go to an engagement in the depths of rural Suffolk. It was autumn and when I arrived in the area darkness had fallen. I drove into the village half-lost, with only a few sketchy instructions about how to find the house I was looking for. At last I stopped my car and anxiously went up to a darkened front porch in order to ask the way. I knocked on the door, only to find to my great surprise that this was the house where my hosts lived! Although it all ended so well it was a tentative, anxious journey indeed. But, of course, to go there now would be a completely different experience. Now, having been there before, I would be much more confident, much less anxious and more certain of my way. It is like that with the Christian life. The more we put Christ's teaching into practice, the more we find him faithful, the more we find that his promises are true. We find ourselves with the feeling: 'I've been here before!' And as we go on there is a deeper and deeper confidence that we are on the right track. The Christian is someone who, amid a changing world, in which people are often uncertain as they deny the possibility of true direction in life, is able to be certain, assured and confident.

The mature Christian is able to stand with the great people of biblical history and affirm a confident faith. Job said, 'I *know* that my redeemer lives.' The apostle Paul wrote, 'We *know* that in all things God works for the good of those who love him.' What a marvellous thing to have such confidence as we face the trials of life!

## 2. Freedom

Jesus says, 'You will know the truth, and the truth will set you free.' In the context of his words Jesus particularly has in mind freedom with respect to sin, for he goes on to say, 'I tell you the truth, everyone who sins is a slave to sin... So if the Son sets you free, you will be free indeed.' Anyone whose general way of life is the way of sin is a slave to sin. Only Christ can bring freedom.

He sets us free from the *penalty* of sin. As sinners we are guilty of high treason against God the King. We would rather live without God than for God. We are unclean in the sight of a holy God. But as we trust Christ and follow him, his atoning death on the cross applies to us. He died as the substitute for his people. We are cleansed. The eternal death penalty for sin has been dealt with. The price has been paid for us.

He sets us free also from the *power* of sin. This is a progressive work, in which our lives are gradually changed to become more like Jesus. The picture of a boat being towed along a river comes to mind. We are like a boat being pulled in the direction of sin. But as people become Christians, the tow rope of sin has been cut. It no longer governs our life. Now we are in the process of being turned around to follow in the opposite direction. It takes time to turn a boat around. It does not happen immediately. Our lives are a continual process of turning to follow the way of Jesus more perfectly. Before we become Christians our lives are inevitably centred on ourselves. We are slaves to self and sin. We are bound to godless patterns of behaviour. There is deep-seated rebellion. There are deep-seated strategies of self-centredness and self-protection which keep us from being the people God would have us to be. But as the truth of Christ takes hold of us, and takes a stronger and stronger grip, we begin to change. We come to a great awareness of the love of God for us. We find security and soul-satisfaction in his love. We realize that selfishness only impoverishes us and hurts others. We realize that we do not need to live that way any more. 'I don't have to be so careful to protect myself. God protects and provides for me. I can take the risk of loving others, knowing that even if I do get rejected by them, God's love will hold me.' As the Holy Spirit gives us strength we are thus enabled to move away from the patterns of sin into a real life of love. The power of sin is broken. We are set free to be the people we ought to be.

He sets us free, too, from the *pain* of sin. We were made in the image of God, but this fallen world has squeezed us into its mould and we have willingly gone along with it. The world has distorted our lives and brought great pain. As an example of this many of us can think of the pain that the idea of 'free love' which has swept over the West in the last thirty years has brought. There are so many heart-broken children of divorces who are distanced from their true father or mother. There are other children who have been abused by parents and stepparents. Sin brings pain and many of us are victims of the hurt that it brings in various ways. But now as we put the past behind us and follow Christ, we find ourselves bring remade. The influence of God's Spirit, the assimilation of God's truth and the experience of God's love begin to soothe our wounded lives and bring us peace. His love frees us from the bitterness, disillusionment and resentment about life which sin forces upon people. We begin to find peace. Christ has set us free.

Just as a plant needs the proper soil, the right temperature and the most congenial environment in which to flourish, so the truth of God is the perfect environment for the human spirit to grow and find fulfilment. As we follow God's ways, receive his forgiveness and enjoy his marvellous love, we flourish as personalities. We find ourselves truly free.

## God's one world

Commitment to Christ does not just have results for the individual; there is a wonderfully wide social dimension.

## The road to freedom

We began this book by thinking about the modern-day drive towards one world. God, too, has that goal in mind. He is about the business of building a new world. Through the Lord Jesus Christ's work on the cross and the regenerating work of the Holy Spirit in the hearts of individuals, he is preparing people to be a part of that coming new world. Already he is saving people and drawing them together in local churches. The local congregations are families of new life and all part of the one great family of God's redeemed people. The church is the workshop where, under the truth of Christ and with the help of God's Spirit to energize them, people are learning to relate to one another in the way God would have them do. The local congregations are communities of the new life. These congregations have persisted down all the years of Christian history and now are proliferating all over the earth. In every land there are growing communities founded on the truth and love of Jesus Christ. The invitation goes out to all the earth to come to faith in Christ and become a part of God's family which will one day inherit a new heaven and a new earth.

Jesus said, 'Blessed are the meek, for they will inherit the earth' (Matthew 5:5). What men long for, but can never achieve on their own, God will achieve through his Son Jesus. There will be a new world where people are brought together in love and unity and freedom for ever. Will you turn to Christ and be part of God's great plan? Paul, the apostle has written, 'He [God] made known to us the mystery of his will according to his good pleasure, which he purposed in Christ, to be put into effect when the times will have reached their fulfilment — to bring all things in heaven and on earth together under one head, even Christ' (Ephesians 1:9-10).

The last book of the Bible, the mysterious book of Revelation which looks into the future and into heaven, brings before us a marvellous and heart-warming scene of God's one world. John, the writer, describes what he saw: 'I looked and there before me was a great multitude that no one could count, from every nation, tribe, people and language, standing before the throne and in front of the Lamb. They were wearing white robes and were holding palm branches in their hands. And they cried out with a loud voice:

> "'Salvation belongs to our God,
> who sits on the throne,
> and to the Lamb'"
>
> (Revelation 7:9-10).

This same book of Revelation closes with a wonderful vision of one great city where all the redeemed people are one with God and one with each other: 'Then the angel showed me the river of the water of life, as clear as crystal, flowing from the throne of God and of the Lamb down the middle of the great street of the city. On each side of the river stood the tree of life, bearing twelve crops of fruit, yielding its fruit every month. And the leaves of the tree are for the healing of the nations. No longer will there be any curse. The throne of God and of the Lamb will be in the city, and his servants will serve him' (Revelation 22:1-3).

We are all invited to be there: 'The Spirit and the bride say, "Come!" And let him who hears say, "Come!" Whoever is thirsty, let him come; and whoever wishes, let him take the free gift of the water of life' (Revelation 22:17).

# Appendix I

### The Bible's attitude to other religions

Sometimes the impression can be given that for biblical faith to compete with other religions is a fairly new occurrence which has only arisen out of the close ties of the modern world. People were brought up in one country and did not know much about what other people believed and therefore did not question their own faith in the light of other religions. This actually is complete nonsense. Even a most cursory reading of the story which the Bible unfolds shows that throughout its whole development biblical faith has had to face the challenge of many other rivals, from the gods of Mesopotamia in Abraham's day right through to the intellectual subtleties of Greek philosophy of the early Christian era. The faith of the Bible emerged not as some closely protected hot-house plant forever protected against the storms, but it grew and won out on the open field of real life. Here we briefly review how the contenders to biblical faith are viewed in the Bible.

### 1. The origin of religion

The idea of an evolution of religious ideas, from the primitive animistic, tribal religions through to the more sophisticated world faiths, is often held. But this view of religious development is not the biblical view, nor does it seem to fit with the facts.

The Bible begins with the story of Adam and Eve, who knew God but rejected him. It speaks more of a deterioration of religion than of an upward evolution. The apostle Paul, giving his great exposition of the Christian faith in the New Testament book of Romans, writes, 'For although they knew God, they neither glorified him as God nor gave thanks to him, but their thinking became futile and their foolish hearts were darkened. Although they claimed to be wise, they became fools and exchanged the glory of the immortal God for images made to look like mortal man and birds and animals and reptiles' (Romans 1:21-23).

The evidence concerning so-called primal religions from modern research seems, too, to be more easily explained by the assumption that this form of religion has developed (or degenerated) as the Bible would indicate, from an original worship of the one Creator — God.

Robert Brow writes, 'Led by Fr. Willhelm Schmidt of Vienna, anthropologists have shown that the religion of the hundreds of isolated tribes in the world today is not primitive in the sense of being original. The tribes have a memory of a "High God", who is no longer worshipped because he is not feared. Instead of offering sacrifice to him, they concern themselves with the pressing problems of how to appease the vicious spirits of the jungle. The threats of the witch-doctor are more strident than the still, small voice of the Father-God.

'We see, then, that the evolution of religion from a primitive animism can no longer be assumed as axiomatic and that some anthropologists now suggest that monotheism may be more naturally primitive as a world-view than animism. Their research suggests that tribes are not animistic because they have continued unchanged since the dawn of history. Rather, the evidence indicates degeneration from a true knowledge of

God. Isolation from prophets and religious books has ensnared them into sacrificial bribery to placate the spirits instead of joyous sacrificial meals in the presence of the Creator.'

## 2. The milieu of idolatry

It is because God was originally known by mankind that wrong ideas about God and wrong worship of him are viewed as sin. The first two of God's Ten Commandments to his people, the nation of Israel, deal with this matter: 'You shall have no other gods before me. You shall not make for yourself an idol in the form of anything in heaven above or on the earth beneath or in the waters below' (Exodus 20:3-4).

It is interesting to note that Abraham, the father of the Jewish nation, and the spiritual father of all who trust the God revealed in Scripture, was called and came to know God out of a background of idolatry: 'Joshua said to all the people, "This is what the Lord, the God of Israel, says: 'Long ago your forefathers, including Terah the father of Abraham and Nahor, lived beyond the River and worshipped other gods'"' (Joshua 24:2-3). 'To this he replied: "Brothers and fathers, listen to me! The God of glory appeared to our father Abraham while he was still in Mesopotamia, before he lived in Haran. 'Leave your country and your people,' God said, 'and go to the land I will show you'"' (Acts 7:2-3).

Abraham was a worshipper of idols, lifeless wooden and stone images, but to his great astonishment and joy the living God found him. Throughout Israel's history the God of Abraham's descendants is characterized by the fact that he is the *living* God, whereas the gods of the nations are dead, mere figments of human imagination, or worse still, manifestations of demonic realities. The prophet Isaiah points up these matters:

> 'Remember the former things, those of long ago;
>> I am God, and there is no other;
>> I am God, and there is none like me.
> I make known the end from the beginning,
>> from ancient times, what is still to come.
> I say: My purpose will stand,
>> and I will do all that I please'
>
> (Isaiah 46:9-10).

In the days when Israel was divided into two nations, Israel and Judah, the people fell into worshipping the 'god' Baal. But at Mount Carmel Elijah, the prophet of God, challenged the prophets of Baal to a contest, to see who was the true God. A sacrifice was offered and the God who answered by sending fire from heaven would be deemed the true God. To the prayers of the devotees of Baal there was no answer, but in answer to Elijah's prayer the sacrifice was consumed by heavenly fire. The people knew that day that the Lord is the true God. This is just one example of how the Lord showed himself to be the true God and the idols to be false. Perhaps the greatest demonstration of this was at the Exodus. In one sense the bringing of God's people out from slavery in Egypt was viewed as a contest between the Lord and the gods of Egypt, who were totally unable to protect the Egyptians from the plagues which the Lord sent.

It is not just that idolatry is viewed as wrong; it is also that it inevitably leads to bad effects on the people who worship false gods. This is how the psalmist puts it:

> 'Our God is in heaven;
>> he does whatever pleases him.
> But their idols are silver and gold,
>> made by the hands of men.
> They have mouths, but cannot speak,
>> eyes but they cannot see;

> they have ears, but cannot hear,
>> noses, but they cannot smell;
> they have hands, but cannot feel,
>> feet, but they cannot walk;
>> nor can they utter a sound with their throats.
> Those who make them will be like them,
>> and so will all who trust in them'
>
> (Psalm 115:3-8).

All who follow false idols will be as spiritually lifeless as the dead idols themselves. Without the living worship of the true God in our souls, religion inevitably becomes grim and futile. It was for this reason that, while staying in ancient Athens and seeing there all the idols and temples of the gods, the apostle Paul, out of love for people, was moved to preach the gospel: 'While Paul was waiting for them in Athens, he was greatly distressed to see that the city was full of idols. So he reasoned in the synagogue with the Jews and the God-fearing Greeks, as well as in the market-place day by day with those who happened to be there' (Acts 17:16-17).

## 3. Israel's destruction of the peoples of Canaan

When, after the exodus from Egypt, God led his people into the promised land, he gave them instructions to destroy utterly all the people there who worshipped other gods. On the surface this might be assessed as unnecessarily harsh. However, there are two things to be borne in mind, which provide us with more understanding as to why God said this must be done.

Firstly, the destruction of the followers of other gods in Canaan was not an arbitrary act, nor was it arbitrarily timed. All idolatry leads, not only to spiritual deadness, but also to human cruelty. The Bible sees life as a whole and wrong ideas about God and wrong worship will inevitably bring about a loss of human dignity and cruel practices. When God first promised Abraham that his descendants would possess the land of Canaan he explained why they would wait a number of generations before the time was right for this: 'In the fourth generation your descendants will come back here, for the sin of the Amorites has not yet reached its full measure' (Genesis 15:16).

By the time of the Exodus the people of Canaan, led on by their worship of idols, were indulging in the most vile and cruel of practices, including the ritual sacrifice of little children to their pagan gods. The idolatry of Canaan had led to sadistic oppression and brutality. If the modern world would justify, say, the Second World War against Nazism by saying that the holocaust of the concentration camps had to be stopped, then in just the same way, in God's eyes, the cruelty of Canaan had to be stopped, and he used his own nation, Israel, to do that.

Secondly, Israel's entry into Canaan was not just an act of judgement. It was also a link in the chain of salvation. There God's people would settle and it was to be through his people Israel that God would eventually send the Messiah, the Lord Jesus Christ, to be the Saviour of the world. If the Messiah was to come and his work was to be properly rooted and understood, it was essential that God's people, the Jews, be grounded in the truth concerning God. It was essential that true religion, as it had been revealed up to that time, be established and preserved among them. It was essential that God's laws be understood, that the seriousness of sin and the need for blood atonement for sin be settled firmly in the consciousness of the nation. It was essential that through the ups and downs of Israel's life the need for the Messiah to come should be clearly seen. Thus true religion, the pure revelation of God's truth, had to be preserved at all costs. God was aware of the tendency of the human heart to drift away from him, so he insisted that his people Israel be pure. God himself is holy. If his people were not holy it would be totally incongruous. Christ had to come into a nation that knew the truth of holiness. So God insisted that all traces of the defiling and abominable idolatry of Canaan be totally obliterated from the land in order to give his people a clean start in their life for him. The constant tendency down the years of Old Testament history for Israel to go after other gods only points up the necessity of God's action against Canaan.

## 4. A spectrum of attitudes

There is always a strident insistence upon the uniqueness of Israel's God as the only true God and therefore an inherent rejection of all other ways. But the Bible reveals a spectrum of attitudes to those of other faiths.

In the first place, the gross idolatry and sinful practices of debauched paganism are utterly condemned and rejected. Those who worship the creature rather than the Creator are bound for judgement (Romans 1:21-24).

However, there is also alongside this a more benevolent attitude to 'the sincere seeker' of other faiths. The Bible sees a general revelation of God in the creation. There is a light which shines on all men and declares the glory of God (Psalm 19:1-4). And God has set this revelation in the world, in the words of the apostle Paul, 'that men would seek him and perhaps reach out for him and find him, though he is not far from each one of us' (Acts 17:27). In creation there is that which points towards the true and living God, and although this is in itself insufficient to lead people to salvation (Romans 10:14), yet it can be used by God to stir people up to seek him and if this should be God's will, to lead them to Jesus.

So it is that we find in Scripture evidence of God's kindly dealings with devout pagans. Their religion is insufficient to save them, but they are led on by God into the truth. Only Jesus can provide true revelation, redemption and regeneration, and people must come to him alone for salvation. Nevertheless there is a benevolence towards, and a recognition of the sincerity and piety of, some people of other religions which the Christian does well to note.

To see this one could think of the wise men, the Magi, who were mysteriously led by the star to the manger of Bethlehem to find the Messiah. Their initial beliefs were insufficient: they had to come to Jesus. Yet God met them in their former state and led them on.

Similarly, towards the end of Jesus' ministry certain Greeks came seeking to talk to Jesus (John 12:20-22) and our Lord took this as a sign that the hour for his crucifixion had come. A number of the Church Fathers saw this as evidence that a positive searching after truth, in the tradition of the Greek philosophers, could be used to lead people to Jesus.

Again it was while the Roman centurion Cornelius was outside of Christ and still on the edge of Judaism, that God sent his angel to this sincere man in order to tell him to invite the apostle Peter to come and preach to the people of his house (Acts 10:1-6).

But while we see in these instances the benevolence of God towards sincere folk of other faiths, the Scriptures nevertheless insist on only one way of salvation.

'For there is one God and one mediator between God and men, the man Christ Jesus' (1 Timothy 2:5).

# Appendix II

**The coming of the man of lawlessness**

As the world changes, we naturally think about what the future holds. How will the world develop? What is God's plan for history? The Bible tells us that the world will end with the second coming of Christ and the transformation of all things. But what will happen in the run-up to that last great event? The apostle Paul wrote a letter to the Christians in Thessalonica in which he reveals some interesting facts which may have a bearing on the theme we have taken up in this book.

> 'Concerning the coming of our Lord Jesus Christ and our being gathered to him, we ask you, brothers, not to become easily unsettled or alarmed by some prophecy, report or letter supposed to have come from us, saying that the day of the Lord has already come. Don't let anyone deceive you in any way, for that day will not come until the rebellion occurs and the man of lawlessness is revealed, the man doomed to destruction. He will oppose and will exalt himself over everything that is called God or is worshipped, so that he sets himself up in God's temple, proclaiming himself to be God.
> 
> 'Don't you remember that when I was with you I used to tell you these things? And now you know what is holding him back, so that he may be revealed at the

proper time. For the secret power of lawlessness is already at work; but the one who now holds it back will continue to do so till he is taken out of the way. And then the lawless one will be revealed, whom the Lord Jesus will overthrow with the breath of his mouth and destroy by the splendour of his coming. The coming of the lawless one will be in accordance with the work of Satan displayed in all kinds of counterfeit miracles, signs and wonders, and in every sort of evil that deceives those who are perishing. They perish because they refused to love the truth and so be saved. For this reason God sends them a powerful delusion so that they will believe the lie and so that all will be condemned who have not believed the truth but have delighted in wickedness.

'But we ought always to thank God for you, brothers loved by the Lord, because from the beginning God chose you to be saved through the sanctifying work of the Spirit and through belief in the truth. He called you to this through our gospel, that you might share in the glory of our Lord Jesus Christ. So then, brothers, stand firm and hold to the teachings we passed on to you, whether by word of mouth or by letter.

'May our Lord Jesus Christ himself and God our Father, who loved us and by his grace gave us eternal encouragement and good hope, encourage your hearts and strengthen you in every good deed and word' (2 Thessalonians 2:1-17).

We will just pick out some of the leading ideas in this passage of Scripture and comment on them.

The Thessalonian church was being unsettled by rumours and 'prophecies' that said that Christ had already somehow returned (vv. 1-2). 'If so,' they were saying to themselves, 'where is he?' 'What about the judgement and the new heavens and the new earth? Or is Christianity a lie? Might we just as

## Appendix II

well give up being Christians?' Historically rumours and ideas such as these have plagued the church from time to time and the first-century church was no different. In their alarm and unsettled condition Paul wrote this chapter to the Thessalonian Christians to calm them down. In doing so, he sets out something of God's timetable for the events leading up to the true return of Christ. He says, 'Don't let anyone deceive you in any way, for that day [the day of the Lord's return] will not come until the rebellion occurs and the man of lawlessness is revealed, the man doomed to destruction' (v. 3).

Before the coming of Jesus there is to be a 'rebellion' which will be such a striking phenomenon that it will be a recognizable signpost to the coming of Jesus. Paul is not talking about a political rebellion, or revolution, but he is talking about moral rebellion. This is plain from the fact that this rebellion will climax in the appearing and rise to power of a man who is characterized by 'lawlessness'.

As we observe the moral breakdown of our society and the throwing off of the law of God from public life, we should remember Paul's teaching. Obviously there have been periods of decadence in many societies throughout history and often those periods have led into the collapse of those societies. We must not be too quick therefore to identify what is happening today with the final 'rebellion' of which Paul speaks, but on the other hand we must not be too quick to dismiss the idea that it might be so.

One new factor in the equation, however, is the advent of TV and cinema in the twentieth century, and their effects upon people. In 1989 the journalist Tom Davies, formerly the *Observer* diarist Pendennis, published a very interesting study[1] entitled *The Man of Lawlessness*. In that book he documents what he sees as the power of the modern mass-media in stimulating the lawless attitudes of our day. The electronic screen has the power to speak to the whole world and bring evil right into the home. He is prepared to link this whole threat to society to Paul's words here in 2 Thessalonians.

Time will tell and the Christian is called to be awake to these things and to 'watch' (Matthew 24:42; 25:13). We are not to try to speculate on precise times and dates for Christ's return. Jesus warned us against that, but we are to be spiritually awake and to know what to expect.

Now what Paul has to say about the precursors to the coming of Christ centres around this figure he calls 'the man of lawlessness', whose coming is identifiable to the watching Christian and will precede the return of Jesus. If we read other extracts of Paul's teaching on this matter, his thought seems to be that in the 'last times' (the time between Christ's first and second comings) there will be a mounting manifestation of sin and wickedness inspired by the powers of evil (see 1 Timothy 4:1-3; 2 Timothy 3:1-9; see also Matthew 24:10-31). Here he is saying that a feature of the climax of this rebellion will be 'the man of lawlessness' (v. 3). In the verses in 2 Thessalonians Paul covers his coming three times, bringing out three different aspects. He speaks of his dominance, his destiny and his deceitfulness.

## His dominance (vv. 3-4)

This figure is a man, not just a concept. That is the plain meaning of Paul's words. He will come to a worldwide position of dominance, especially in the religious sphere.

### He will be revealed

That points to his existence before his manifestation. So he will suddenly come into the limelight from out of the shadows, as it were. The word 'revealed' used here is the same one that is used earlier by Paul in the same letter (2 Thessalonians 1:7) to describe the second coming of Jesus. So there may be some kind of pseudo-parallel between the two, and something supernatural about the appearance of this man. Indeed verse 9 speaks about counterfeit miracles which relate to his coming.

# Appendix II

It is difficult to say who this man of lawlessness is or will be. Again, we realize that throughout history there have been many evil men who have done Satan's work — Hitler and Stalin in our own century. In biblical terminology, there have been many 'antichrists' (1 John 2:18). So it would be unwise to make an over-hasty identification. Paul is pointing us to the most infamous of them all, who will come just before Christ's true return. The apostle John calls him 'the antichrist'.

He is 'the man doomed to destruction' (v. 3). The original wording of this verse is 'the son of perdition'. That is a term used elsewhere in the New Testament only of Judas Iscariot (John 17:12). Does that help us with our identification of this man? Will he be someone like Judas, who was once a friend of Christianity, but who turns violently against the true faith?

## He will gather all religion and worship around himself

These verses tell us that he will oppose the true faith and will exalt himself over the true God and any so-called god. He will have himself 'exalted above measure' over all kinds of religion and religious practice. In other words, Paul seems to be pointing to a time when all world faiths are gathered into one with this 'man of lawlessness' at the head of it all. This is very interesting in the light of moves in the religious world over the last fifty years. As our world has shrunk by the benefits of supersonic air travel and telecommunications, many barriers have come down and there is greater understanding between people, which is a good thing. But the pressure is for all religions to sink their differences. Multi-faith conferences are called, and some people would like to see an umbrella world religion. The pope himself has chaired such a multi-faith gathering. The New Age Movement has much influence in the corridors of the United Nations and in many multi-national companies.

Paul's words here are reminiscent of the words of Jesus in

Mark 13:14: 'When you see "the abomination that causes desolation" standing where it does not belong [in the temple, see Daniel 9:27; 11:31] — let the reader understand — then let those who are in Judea flee to the mountains.' Here Jesus is primarily talking about the destruction of Jerusalem in A.D. 70 by the Roman armies, but in the rest of the passage he goes on to talk about his own second coming, in such a way as to lead us to think that the destruction of Jerusalem was somehow a pattern for the end of the world. What happened in A.D. 70 gives us clues concerning his own second coming. In A.D. 70 the Roman armies defiled and destroyed the Jerusalem temple. Paul says of the man of lawlessness that he will 'set himself up in God's temple'. Does that mean a physical building? Or is Paul using the imagery he often uses, speaking of the temple to refer to the church? Will this man take over the establishment church? That is not to say that the gospel will not continue to grow where local churches and fellowships remain faithful to Scripture. But these will become more and more rejected. The churches may grow in size and number, but there will be mounting polarization and antagonism between Bible-believing faith and world religion. Is this the way in which our times are going?

The underlying trend in the emergence of the man of lawlessness is to give religious sanction to sin. Sin is lawlessness, the rejection of God's law. The move will be towards the sweeping away of all absolutes of lifestyle and moral behaviour, under the cloak of a worldwide, beneficent religion, which declares, 'Live as you like. It is for each person to find his or her own way,' and smiles upon all.

**His destiny** (vv. 5-8)

Paul runs over this matter again. But this time his emphasis is on the fact that although the coming of the man of lawlessness will seem very frightening and unnerving for the Christian at the time, it is all in God's control. The Lord is only working out his plan. This very frightening figure is actually only playing out a role which God has given him. He will come only at his appointed time (v. 6) — the time appointed by God. He will fulfil the destiny which God has mapped out for him.

The fact that *he is under God's control* is also underlined by the way Paul refers to him as being 'held back' (v. 6). Similarly in verse 7 he says, 'For the secret power of lawlessness is already at work; but the one who now holds it back will continue to do so till he is taken out of the way.' You see, he is in God's power, on God's leash, all the time.

What is Paul referring to when he speaks of that which holds back the man of lawlessness? The Thessalonians knew (vv. 5-6) and Paul knew, but unfortunately it is not very clear to us. There are many ideas among Bible commentators as to what Paul is referring to. Some say it is the restraining work of the Holy Spirit in the world. Others suggest that it could be the principle of law and order enshrined in the Roman government of the day, which same principle has come down to us today. Many of the principles generally accepted in Western states are still based on the Roman ideas of law.

There is an argument that Paul could be referring to the influence of the Scriptures themselves. There are a number of things to note in relation to this idea. Firstly, he speaks of the restraint both as a thing (v. 6) and as a person (v. 7). Secondly, it is interesting that in the rest of the letter Paul speaks in terms of 'us', that is, Paul, Silas and Timothy, who are writing the letter. But here he speaks only of himself (v. 5). Paul is one of the foundational apostles of Christ. Indeed he is *the* apostle to the Gentiles and his authority over the church and the authority of Scripture are one and the same. As one of the authoritative writers of Scripture, is Paul here, in his self-deprecating way, referring to himself and his teaching, the Scriptures? Generally speaking, the great move by the world over the last 200 years has been to attack the Scriptures. There seems to be a mood, not just to ask reasonable questions of Scripture and seek reasonable answers, which is a good thing, but a desire to throw off the Bible and get rid of its influence and its conscience-pricking truth. Is it that once the institutional church has finally thrown over all pretence of submission to Scripture, having 'disproved the Bible', the stage will then be clear for the unity of faiths and a free-for-all in religion and the arrival of the man of lawlessness? But whatever the actual means God uses to hold back this man, the point not to be missed is that what happens is never outside God's control. God's plans are working out.

This figure will arrive on the world scene one day, but only in God's timing. When he does faithful Christians are not to be overwhelmed and discouraged. All this has to happen. It may seem as if all is up with the cause of Christ. Despite the growth of the numbers of faithful Christians through worldwide mission, the point may come where it seems as if the world will destroy all true Christianity. But it will not happen, for *God has appointed this man to a destiny of destruction.* Christ will suddenly come and rescue his church: 'And then the lawless one will be revealed, whom the Lord Jesus will overthrow with the breath of his mouth and destroy by the splendour of his coming' (v. 8). He will be blown away in judgement.

Christians will be saved, the true church will be saved, not by a gradual conquering of the world (although many people will be converted), but by divine intervention. Christ will unexpectedly arrive at just the time when the world thinks he can finally be ignored and forgotten and they can get on with life without any reference to him.

So we may well observe the world going from bad to worse, and biblical faith suffering what may seem to be reversals of various kinds along with a growth by mission. Increasingly there may be difficulties and antagonism towards Christ's followers. But all this is part of the road leading to Christ's return.

## His deceitfulness (vv. 9-12)

The theologian Geerhardus Vos says of the man of lawlessness, 'His activity lies fundamentally in the sphere of religious and moral seduction.' That is clear from these verses. He comes to 'deceive' (v. 10). Associated with him there will be 'a powerful delusion' (v. 11). He comes to try to beguile people away from worship of Christ and to seduce them into corrupt living. How does he do this?

Over the last thirty years or so, we have seen the rise in the church of the expectation of miracles and the supernatural intervention of God. There has been much focus on things like healing ministries, and it is true that some wonderful things have happened.

However, sadly, it has led to a dangerous mentality among some Christians. This mentality is that 'If something miraculous happens it is good and is of God. If there are no miracles God is not at work and it is useless.' That is in fact a highly dangerous approach, for when the man of lawlessness comes, there will be plenty of miracles. 'The coming of the lawless one will be in accordance with the work of Satan displayed in all kinds of counterfeit miracles, signs and wonders' (v. 9). He will work in the power of Satan as Christ did in the power of the Holy Spirit, and he will perform miracles of various kinds as did the Lord. These 'counterfeit miracles' are not bogus tricks. That is not the meaning. They are real miracles, but they produce false impressions. They lead people away from the truth. God will allow this to happen (vv. 10,11) because it will purge the church. It will distinguish those who do not really love the truth from those who do. It will expose those who are in religion for the excitement, but whose natures have never been changed and show who really loves Christ and who does not. It will sift out the true from the false.

Please do not get me wrong. I am all for the powerful and miraculous working of the Holy Spirit. But his miracles are those which lead people to Christ, and to godliness and to submission to the Lord and his Word in Scripture. Where that happens, fine! But this is different. These will be miracles which lead people into saying we must not be too strong on the uniqueness of Christ, or Jesus as the only way to God. These will be wonders that lead people away from the discipline of Christlike holiness, away from the authority of the Bible. We need to be discerning. The mentality which quickly equates any miracles with the work of God, and despises any lack of the miraculous, is highly dangerous. It is a mentality which the man of lawlessness could easily exploit. The miraculous alone is no guarantee of the true work of God. The man of lawlessness is a deceiver and he comes to lead people away from the truth.

**Be alert!** (vv. 13-15)

However, Paul tells us that Christians who are awake will see through all this and stand for Christ.

We have seen the dominance, the destiny and the deceitfulness of the man of lawlessness. Are we beginning to see the arrival of these things in our day? We cannot be certain. But as we see the way the world is going and as we hear different rumours, how are we to keep our bearings? There are two things in verses 13-15 on which to keep our eyes.

How are people saved? By *the sanctifying work of the Holy Spirit* (v.13). It is not necessarily by the miraculous work the Spirit can produce, but by the holiness and the Christlikeness that he produces in people's lives. That is the fruit of the Spirit. That is the mark of salvation. Do not let yourself ever lose sight of that fact. In all the ups and downs and changes in the world and in the church scene, keep your eye on Christlike, loving holiness. Wherever it is found, this is authentic Christianity, whether there are miracles or not.

How are people saved? Through *belief in the truth* (v. 13). What is the truth? 'Our gospel,' says Paul (v. 14). We have

*Appendix II*

Paul's gospel, which he preached with Silas and Timothy, today. We have it in the Bible. The truth that Paul loved and preached we have in the printed writings of Paul in Scripture.

Amid all the lawlessness and seductions of the world, amid all the confusion and rumours in the church, we are to look to Scripture, and submit to that. This is the same advice Paul later gave to Timothy as he sought to lead a church in difficult times (2 Timothy 3:14-4:5). The truth of Scripture is the star by which we are to steer our course in the dark night of a fallen world.

Follow Scripture and holiness and you will not go wrong.

# References

**Chapter 2**
1. Lesslie Newbigin, *The gospel in a pluralistic society*, SPCK.
2. *The Surrey Advertizer*, May 1989.
3. R. C. Sproul, *Questions answered*, G/L Publications.

**Chapter 3**
1. Bel Mooney, *The Listener*, 10 April 1986.
2. Quoted by Stephen Neill, *The supremacy of Jesus*, Hodder and Stoughton.

**Chapter 4**
1. Victor Hugo, *Les misérables*.

**Chapter 5**
1. Quoted by Colin Chapman, *The case for Christianity*, Lion.
2. *Ibid.*
3. Quoted by James Montgomery Boice, *Foundations of the Christian faith*, IVP.

**Chapter 6**
1. D. H. Lawrence, *Cypruses*.
2. D. H. Lawrence, *Fantasia of the unconscious*.
3. Trevor Partridge, Institute in Christian Counselling, CWR.

**Appendix II**
1. Tom Davies, *The man of lawlessness*, Hodder & Stoughton.